Developing Windows Store Apps with HTML5 and JavaScript

Learn the key concepts of developing Windows Store apps using HTML5 and JavaScript

Rami Sarieddine

PUBLISHING

BIRMINGHAM - MUMBAI

Developing Windows Store Apps with HTML5 and JavaScript

First published: August 2013

Production Reference: 1160813

Published by Packt Publishing Ltd.
Livery Place
35 Livery Street
Birmingham B3 2PB, UK.

ISBN 978-1-84968-710-2

www.packtpub.com

Cover Image by Michel Makhoul (makhoul.michel@live.com)

Credits

Author
Rami Sarieddine

Reviewers
Nidal Arabi
Juri Strumpflohner
Jenil Vasani

Acquisition Editor
Kevin Colaco

Commissioning Editor
Priyanka Shah

Lead Technical Editor
Ankita Shashi

Technical Editors
Ruchita Bhansali
Jalasha D'costa
Menza Mathew

Project Coordinator
Kranti Berde

Copy Editors
Mradula Hegde
Sayanee Mukherjee
Aditya Nair
Alfida Paiva

Proofreader
Stephen Copestake

Indexer
Priya Subramani
Monica Ajmera Mehta

Graphics
Ronak Dhruv

Production Coordinator
Manu Joseph

Cover Work
Manu Joseph

About the Author

Rami Sarieddine is a Technical Evangelist for Windows Azure and Windows 8 with Microsoft Gulf. Prior to joining Microsoft, he was working as a Software Engineer and Analyst at the American University of Beirut. He has a cumulative 7 years of experience in web development. In the span of these 7 years, he started with an independent venture for around 2 years. After that he directly embarked on an employment journey that was rich with experience, during which he had led numerous projects and held several positions from Web Developer to Information Systems Analyst and Lead Web Developer.

He was Microsoft Valued Professional awardee in 2013 and 2012 for his contributions in the technical communities of Visual C# and ASP.NET/IIS respectively. The MVP award is an annual award that recognizes exceptional technology community leaders worldwide who actively share their high quality, real-world expertise with users and Microsoft. With fewer than 5,000 awardees worldwide, Microsoft MVPs represent a highly select group of experts.

He was selected speaker at the first Tech.Days Beirut event by Microsoft Lebanon. Soon after, he had become a regular speaker on training sessions at their main events including Open Door and Tech Days. He has been heavily involved with Microsoft Lebanon's developer communities and activities, delivering hands-on workshops on Windows 8, HTML5, Azure, and Visual Studio. His passion for pursuing knowledge and experience, and consequently sharing it with fellow web developers and enthusiasts drove him into starting his own technical blog.

When not working, he enjoys running and spending time with his loved ones. And when on vacations, he enjoys traveling and visiting new places around the world.

He can be reached at `r.sarieddine@live.com` and you can follow his articles and blog posts on `http://code4word.com`.

Acknowledgments

Apart from the hard work put into researching and writing, the realization of this book would not have been possible without my publisher Packt Publishing, and the efforts of their Acquisition Editor, the team of Technical Editors, and Proof Readers in helping to complete the book. I would like to express my appreciation and gratitude to the Project Coordinator, Kranti Berde, and the Lead Technical Editor, Ankita Shashi, for their contribution and guidance.

Moreover, I wish to acknowledge Microsoft Lebanon for providing me with the opportunity of delivering training sessions on Windows 8, which contributed to my experience on the subject matter. I would like to express my gratitude for my friend and creative UI designer Michel Makhoul for his work on the cover image. I also wish to express my appreciation for the people who supported me throughout this journey, namely, my colleague Chukri Soueidi for providing me with technical advice and encouragement and my technical mentor Firas Hamdan for his contribution to my knowledge and professional advice.

I would also like to take this opportunity to thank my family who supported my efforts while writing the book.

Above all, I want to express my appreciation and to thank my loved one Elissar Mezher for believing in me, supporting and ever motivating me, and mostly for understanding my long nights at work. Thank you.

About the Reviewers

Nidal Arabi is a Software Engineer graduate of computer science from Lebanese American University in Lebanon, Beirut. He has worked in several companies in the banking sector as well as in the technology sector. He has been designated as Microsoft ASP.NET MVP and he has also written many articles on ASP Alliance website. He has experience in different technologies ranging from Java to .NET.

> I would like to thank my wife Nivine Jundi for supporting me and providing the time to review the book.

Juri Strumpflohner currently works as a Software Architect for an e-government company, where his main responsibility is to coach developers to create appealing rich client web applications with HTML5, JavaScript, and the .NET technology stack. If you're interested in web development and best practices in software development, you can visit his website at `juristr.com`, where he actively blogs about such topics. He also participates in online communities such as StackOverflow, and on open source projects on GitHub. When he is not in front of his computer, he is probably practicing Yoseikan Budo where he currently owns a 2nd DAN. He holds a degree of Master of Science in Computer Science.

Jenil Vasani has completed Engineering in Information Technology from Atharva College of Engineering. He is a tech enthusiast, developer, and Microsoft Student Partner, Gamer, and Blogger.

I would like to express my special thanks of gratitude to my parents, God, and Packt Publishing who gave me the opportunity to review this book. This book has helped me in doing a lot of research. I would also like to thank my friends who contributed their suggestions.

www.PacktPub.com

Support files, eBooks, discount offers and more

You might want to visit www.PacktPub.com for support files and downloads related to your book.

Did you know that Packt offers eBook versions of every book published, with PDF and ePub files available? You can upgrade to the eBook version at www.PacktPub.com and as a print book customer, you are entitled to a discount on the eBook copy. Get in touch with us at service@packtpub.com for more details.

At www.PacktPub.com, you can also read a collection of free technical articles, sign up for a range of free newsletters, and receive exclusive discounts and offers on Packt books and eBooks.

http://PacktLib.PacktPub.com

Do you need instant solutions to your IT questions? PacktLib is Packt's online digital book library. Here you can access, read, and search across Packt's entire library of books.

Why Subscribe?
- Fully searchable across every book published by Packt
- Copy and paste, print, and bookmark content
- On demand and accessible via web browser

Free Access for Packt account holders

If you have an account with Packt at www.PacktPub.com, you can use this to access PacktLib today and view nine entirely free books. Simply use your login credentials for immediate access.

Instant Updates on New Packt Books

Get notified! Find out when new books are published by following @PacktEnterprise on Twitter, or the *Packt Enterprise* Facebook page.

Table of Contents

Preface

Developing Windows Store Apps with HTML5 and JavaScript is a practical, hands-on guide that covers the basic and important features of a Windows Store app along with code examples that will show you how to develop these features, all the while learning some of the new features in HTML5 and CSS3, which allows you to leverage your web development skills.

What this book covers

Chapter 1, HTML5 Structure, presents an introduction to the new Semantic elements, Media elements, Form elements, and Custom data attributes in the new HTML5 specs.

Chapter 2, Styling with CSS3, introduces the new enhancements and features introduced by CSS3 that will be frequently needed when developing a Windows Store app with JavaScript. This chapter covers the following topics: CSS3 Selectors, Grid and Flexbox, Animation and Transforms, and Media Queries.

Chapter 3, JavaScript for Windows Apps, covers the Windows Library for JavaScript and its features, as well as highlighting the namespaces and controls used for developing the apps.

Chapter 4, Developing Apps with JavaScript, covers the tools needed and the templates provided to get started with developing a Windows 8 app using JavaScript.

Chapter 5, Binding Data to the App, describes how to implement data binding in an app.

Chapter 6, Making the App Responsive, describes how to make the app responsive so that it handles screen sizes and view state changes and responds to zooming in and out.

Chapter 7, Making the App Live with Tiles and Notifications, describes the concept of app tiles and notifications, and how to create a simple notification for an app.

Chapter 8, Signing Users in, describes the Live Connect API and how to integrate the apps with this API to enable user authentication, and sign-on, and retrieve user profile information.

Chapter 9, Adding Menus and Commands, describes the app bar, how it works, and where it is found on the app. Moreover, we will learn how to declare an app bar and add controls to it.

Chapter 10, Packaging and Publishing, covers how we will get introduced to the Store and learn how to get an app through all the stages into publishing. Also, we will see how we can interact with the Store from within Visual Studio.

Chapter 11, Developing Apps with XAML, describes the other platforms and programming languages that are available for developers. We will also cover the basics of creating an app with XAML/C#.

What you need for this book

In order to implement what you will be learning in this book and start developing Windows Store apps, you'll first need Windows 8. Additionally, you'll require the following development tools and toolkits:

- Microsoft Visual Studio Express 2012 for Windows 8 is the tool to build Windows apps. It includes the Windows 8 SDK, Blend for Visual Studio, and project templates.
- Windows App Certification Kit
- Live SDK

Who this book is for

This book is for all developers who want to start creating apps for Windows 8. Also, it targets developers who want to get introduced to the advancements in standards-based web technology with HTML5 and CSS3. Additionally, the book targets web developers who want to leverage their existing skills, code assets in web development, and direct it to building JavaScript apps for the Windows Store. In short, this book is for everyone who wants to learn the basics of developing a Windows Store app.

Conventions

In this book, you will find a number of styles of text that distinguish between different kinds of information. Here are some examples of these styles and an explanation of their meanings.

Code words in text are shown as follows: "The `createGrouped` method creates a grouped projection over a list and takes three function parameters."

A block of code is set as follows:

```
// Get the group key that an item belongs to.
  function getGroupKey(dataItem) {
  return dataItem.name.toUpperCase().charAt(0);
}

// Get a title for a group
  function getGroupData(dataItem) {
  return {
    title: dataItem.name.toUpperCase().charAt(0);
  };
}
```

New terms and **important words** are shown in bold. Words that you see on the screen, in menus or dialog boxes for example, appear in the text like this: "You will be able to set up options for the application UI; one of these options is Supported rotations."

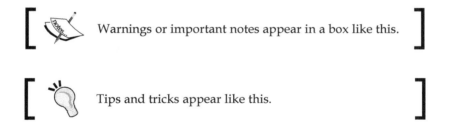

[Warnings or important notes appear in a box like this.]

[Tips and tricks appear like this.]

Reader feedback

Feedback from our readers is always welcome. Let us know what you think about this book—what you liked or may have disliked. Reader feedback is important for us to develop titles that you really get the most out of.

To send us general feedback, simply send an e-mail to feedback@packtpub.com and mention the book title via the subject of your message.

If there is a topic that you have expertise in and you are interested in either writing or contributing to a book, see our author guide on www.packtpub.com/authors.

Customer support

Now that you are the proud owner of a Packt book, we have a number of things to help you to get the most from your purchase.

Errata

Although we have taken every care to ensure the accuracy of our content, mistakes do happen. If you find a mistake in one of our books—maybe a mistake in the text or the code—we would be grateful if you would report this to us. By doing so, you can save other readers from frustration and help us improve subsequent versions of this book. If you find any errata, please report them by visiting http://www.packtpub. com/submit-errata, selecting your book, clicking on the **errata submission form** link, and entering the details of your errata. Once your errata are verified, your submission will be accepted and the errata will be uploaded on our website or added to any list of existing errata, under the Errata section of that title. Any existing errata can be viewed by selecting your title from http://www.packtpub.com/support.

Piracy

Piracy of copyright material on the Internet is an ongoing problem across all media. At Packt, we take the protection of our copyright and licenses very seriously. If you come across any illegal copies of our works, in any form, on the Internet, please provide us with the location address or website name immediately so that we can pursue a remedy.

Please contact us at copyright@packtpub.com with a link to the suspected pirated material.

We appreciate your help in protecting our authors and our ability to bring you valuable content.

Questions

You can contact us at questions@packtpub.com if you are having a problem with any aspect of the book, and we will do our best to address it.

1
HTML5 Structure

HTML5 introduced new elements and attributes for a neater structure, smarter forms, and richer media; this make the life of a developer much easier. HTML5 features are classified into several groups based on their function, and the new structural elements fall under the group semantics, which include structural elements, media elements, attributes, form types, link relation types, semantics for internationalization, and microdata for additional semantics. There is a big list of additions and enhancements in HTML5, all with the aim of better presenting the content on the web. You will use many of these when developing apps for Windows 8; the difference and, moreover, the advantage of using it for Windows 8 development is that you do not have to worry about the browser's compatibility, at least at the level of Windows Store apps, since Windows 8 is an HTML5 platform that uses the most recent web standards. Everything that you use from HTML5 and CSS3 is provided for you in your code and is guaranteed to work in the application. And the latest version of Visual Studio (VS 2012) includes a new HTML and CSS editor that offers full support for HTML5 and CSS3 elements and snippets.

In this chapter we will be covering the following topics:

- Semantic elements
- Media elements
- Form elements
- Custom data attributes

Understanding semantic elements

HTML5 markup is more semantic than its predecessors due to the new semantic elements for describing the structure of the page content. The list of semantic elements includes the following:

- The `<header>` tag defines a header for the document or section. It wraps the heading or a group of headings in a page or a section, and it can also contain information such as logos, banners, and main navigation links. You can have multiple `<header>` tags in a page.

- The `<nav>` tag represents the major navigation links. Typically it is bound to the header.

- The `<section>` tag wraps related content that can be grouped thematically. A `<section>` tag can include a `<header>` and `<footer>` tag.

- The `<footer>` tag represents content about a page or a section, for example, related links, privacy terms, and copyright information. You can have more than one `<footer>` in a page, and it is same as the `<header>` tag.

- The `<article>` tag represents self-contained content that can be used independent of the document as a whole, for example, a blog entry. `<article>` and `<section>` are much alike because both are standalone tags and hold related content; however, if it's content can be syndicated (via an atom or an RSS feed), then the `<article>` element is more appropriate.

- The `<aside>` tag represents the part of a page that is tangentially related to the content around it, and also separate from that content, as it can be removed without affecting the main content of the page. Typical usage can be a sidebar.

- The `<address>` tag represents the contact information for the nearest `<article>` parent element, if present, or the parent `<body>` element, which in that case applies to the whole document.

Putting all these new elements together in a page would yield the following markup:

```
<!DOCTYPE html>
<html lang="en">
<head>
  <meta charset="UTF-8">
  <title>Developing for Windows 8</title>
</head>
<body>
  <header>
```

```html
    <a href="default.html">
      <h1>The Courses</h1>
      <img src="logo.png" alt="Book Logo">
    </a>
    <nav>
      <ul>
        <li><a href="home.html">Home</a></li>
        <li><a href="about.html">About</a></li>
      </ul>
    </nav>
  </header>
  <section>
    <article>
      <h2></h2>
      <p></p>
      <address>
        Written by <a href="mailto:xyz@abc.com">Demo
          Author</a>.<br>
        Found at: Demo.com <br>
        Address, Street<br>
        UK
      </address>
    </article>
    <article>
      <h2></h2>
      <p>content</p>
    </article>
  </section>
  <aside>
    <h2></h2>
    <ul>
      <li></li>
      <li></li>
      <li></li>
    </ul>
    <p></p>
  </aside>
  <footer>
    <p></p>
    <p>Copyright &copy; 2013 Packt</p>
  </footer>
</body>
</html>
```

Introducing built-in media elements

HTML5 introduced new media elements such as <audio> and <video>, which can be considered as a new revolution in media types after images in the earlier versions of HTML. These two elements make it very easy to embed media in your HTML page/document and provide built-in media support via the **HTML5 Media element API**. According to the latest specs by W3C, we can define <video> and <audio> as follows:

- The <video> tag is a media element used for playing videos or movies and audio files with captions
- The <audio> tag is a media element whose media data is audio, that is, a sound or an audio stream

The <audio> and <video> elements play audio and video files respectively. The only difference between them is that the <audio> element does not have a playback area for visual content, contrary to the <video> element.

Prior to HTML5, we needed a plugin in order to play an audio or a video file, and that required writing a large chunk of markup. Without HTML5, embedding media elements was never so easy; just by putting an <audio> tag resulting in two lines of code you can get a media player with playback controls. It is almost the same as the <img /> tag before. Refer to the following code:

```
<audio src="audio.mp3" controls>
</audio>
```

The previous example results in a media player that will look like the following screenshot on Internet Explorer 9 (IE9), and might differ from one browser to another:

The previous code shows the <audio> tag in its simplest form, but the <audio> tag has more attributes and options. Refer to the following code:

```
<audio controls autoplay loop>
  <p>Your browser does not support the audio element. Click <a
href="content/Elsie.mp3"> here </a> to download the file instead.
  </p>
  <source src="audio.mp3" type="audio/mp3" />
  <source src="audio.ogg" type="audio/ogg" />
</audio>
```

First, notice the content wrapped in a `<p>` tag inside the `<audio>` element. This content is a fallback text and will only be used if the browser doesn't support the `<audio>` tag. It provides a graceful fallback for older web browsers by informing the user about this issue, and we can add a link to allow the download of this audio file instead. This way, the user will not just stand there wondering what has happened. This is the simplest way to fallback; you can use JavaScript for the same purpose too.

The preceding code snippet also shows some of the attributes for the `<audio>` element. According to the W3C specification, `src`, `controls`, `autoplay`, `loop`, `preload`, `mediagroup`, and `muted` are common attributes to both the media elements, namely `<audio>` and `<video>`.

- The `controls` attribute displays the standard HTML5 controls for the audio on the webpage, and the design of the controls varies between browser agents.
- The `autoplay` attribute plays the audio file automatically as soon as the DOM finishes loading.
- The `loop` attribute enables repetition automatically.
- The `mediagroup` attribute links multiple media elements together using a media controller.
- The `muted` attribute sets a default state of the audio file to mute.
- The `preload` attribute provides a hint to the user agent about what the author thinks will lead to the best user experience. Its values can be `none`, `metadata`, or `auto`.
  - ° `none`: This value hints to the browser that the web page doesn't expect users to need the media resource.
  - ° `metadata`: This value hints to the browser to fetch the resource metadata (dimensions, track list, duration, and so on).
  - ° `auto`: This value hints to the browser to put the user's needs first without any risk to the server. An empty value, as in just adding the attribute `preload`, maps to the `auto` value.

You can specify a value for the attributes as in `controls="controls"`, which would have the same behavior. But for simplicity and less code, you can simply leave out the value for this attribute; the same can be applied for `loop`, `autoplay`, and `muted`. You can specify the media resource by either using the `src` attribute or the `<source>` elements.

 The attribute overrides the elements.

The media resource (audio or video) has a MIME type and additionally a codec as in the following code:

```
<source src="video.ogv" type="video/ogg; codecs="theora, vorbis" />
```

Setting the value for the `type` attribute has to be done within the `<source>` element. The browser/user agent will avoid downloading the resource if it does not support its type. You can add multiple formats of your audio/video in order to ensure playback support across different browsers. The browser agent will go over the `<source>` elements; if it cannot render the first type, it will skip to the next `<source>` to validate its type, and so on. For this purpose, you will have to check the list of MIME types supported by the `<audio>` and `<video>` elements in different browsers. The browser not only checks for the MIME types but also for the specified codec. So, even if the browser agent can render the resource type, the video/audio will not load if the codec is not supported.

The following table lists the support for the 3 main video formats across the major browsers:

Format	IE9+	Chrome	Firefox	Opera	Safari
WebM (VP8 CODEC)	Yes	Yes	Yes	Yes	No
MP4 (H.264 CODEC)	Yes	Yes	No	No	Yes
OGV (OGG THEORA CODEC)	No	Yes	Yes	Yes	No

From the listing in the previous table, we can conclude that providing a media resource with both WebM and MP4 formats in your HTML5 video will guarantee it to load in the latest versions of all major browsers. This theory is reinforced in Visual Studio 2012, which offers full Intellisense support for HTML5 tags. When you insert the following snippet for an HTML5 `<video>` element, it lists 3 `<source>` elements within the `<video>` tag:

```
<video controls="controls">
  <source src="file.mp4" type="video/mp4" />
  <source src="file.webm" type="video/webm" />
  <source src="file.ogv" type="video/ogg" />
</video>
```

The `<video>` element also includes a `poster` attribute, which is used to specify a path for an image to be displayed in the visual content area when no video data is available or until the user clicks on the play button. For advertising purposes, you can use an image or a frame from the video that gives the user an idea of what the video is like. If you do not specify a poster image and if the `autoplay` attribute is not set, the browser may just display a black box filling the dimensions of the `<video>` element. For example, the following code shows the difference between code samples for two similar videos, with a poster specified for the second video:

```
<video id="video" controls width="400">
  <source
src="http://ie.microsoft.com/testdrive/Videos/BehindIE9AllAroundFast/
video.mp4" type="video/mp4" />
</video>
<video id="videoWithPoster" controls width="400" poster="http://msdn.
microsoft.com/br211386.5_GetStarted_484x272px.jpg">
  <source
src="http://ie.microsoft.com/testdrive/Videos/BehindIE9AllAroundFast/
video.mp4" type="video/mp4" />
</video>
```

The output of this markup will produce the following on the screen:

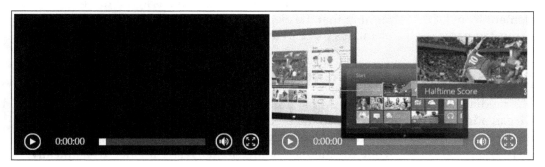

You might have noticed that we specified a `width` value of `400` for the two videos in the previous example. The `<video>` element accepts standard HTML `width` and `height` attributes. If there is no value set for `width` and `height`, the visual content area stretches to the native size of video. It is recommended to set the `width` and `height` attributes on the `<video>` element, thus avoiding stretching to full size, and to encode the video at the desired viewing dimensions.

 The values for the width and height attributes do not accept units. The value indicates CSS pixels, for example, `width=400` is the same as `width=400px`.

There are JavaScript methods, properties, and DOM events that are part of the HTML5 standard that is associated with these new elements. You can read and set properties programmatically, such as the `src` path and the dimensions (`width` and `height`) of the `<video>` tag. You can use JavaScript methods to load the audio and video, and then play and pause the media resource. You can also write code to handle different DOM events raised by media elements, such as `onplaying`, `onprogress` (load progress), `onplay`, and `onpause`. For example, you disable the default controls displayed by the element by removing the `controls` attribute and by calling the functions that play and pause the media resource from separate buttons.

The following code listing shows how we can play and pause the video using JavaScript. We first need to detect the current state of the video file by calling the Boolean property `.paused`, and if true, we then call the methods `play()` or `pause()` accordingly:

```
var testVideo = document.getElementById('myVideo');
if (testVideo.paused)
  testVideo.play();
else
  testVideo.pause();
```

In the preceding code, we declare a variable `testVideo` and assign it to the `myVideo` element from DOM. Assuming that the element was assigned an ID, you can use the name, tag name, or the element's place in the DOM hierarchy to retrieve the elements.

Advanced media with JavaScript

The media elements have a rich API to access with pure JavaScript. Using JavaScript, we can add a lot of functionality to the media elements. You can manipulate the media resource, style it, rotate a video, play two and more media elements in sync, display a progress bar while the media resource loads, resize a video dynamically, and so on.

The following is the code sample that adds functionality to the `timeupdate` event, which fetches the current play time of the video in seconds and displays it in a separate div.

The following is the HTML code:

```
<div id="tInfo"></div>
<video id="myVideo" autoplay controls>
  <source src="w8.mp4" type="video/mp4" />
</video>
```

The following is the JavaScript code:

```
var video = document.getElementsById('myVideo');
var tInfo = document.getElementById('tInfo');
video.addEventListener('timeupdate',function(event){
tInfo.innerHTML = parseInt(video.currentTime);
}, false);
```

The JavaScript `addEventListener` method is used to provide a handler for the `timeupdate` event. It takes three parameters and has the basic syntax, which is as follows:

```
WinJS.Application.addEventListener(type, listener, capture);
```

The `type` parameter specifies the type of event to register, while `listener` is the event handler function to associate with the event, and the third parameter `capture` is a Boolean value that specifies whether the event handler is registered for the capturing phase or not.

In addition, you can combine the capabilities of the `<video>` element with a canvas, allowing you to manipulate video data in real time and add a variety of visual effects.

Introducing feature-rich form elements

Forms and `<form>` elements are an integral part of any application or website, from a login form to a complete contact or registration form. In HTML4, the `<form>` elements were very idle, and for any feature or advanced styling, JavaScript was a necessity. And for any interaction, or data submission and validation, it demanded server and client-side scripting, and its functionality was inhibited if the scripting was disabled in the browser. HTML5 brought major improvements to the `<form>` elements with new attributes and input types, and added features such as browser-based validation and CSS styling that provide a better experience for the users filling it, and all possible simplicity for the developers creating it.

An enriched <input> tag

New values for the `type` attribute are introduced to the `<input>` element.

HTML5 adds 13 new `<input>` types to the ones we were already familiar with in HTML4, such as `text` and `checkbox`. With this addition, the `<input>` control now supports types such as `range`, `date`, `number`, `telephone`, `email`, and `URL`. And these new `<input>` types add intelligent behavior to the element themselves.

The following is the table listing of these types:

`<input>` types	Description
`tel`	It expects a telephone number.
`search`	It prompts the user to enter text that they want to search for, and adds a search icon to the input element (on browsers that support it).
`url`	It expects a single URL.
`email`	It expects a single e-mail address or a list of e-mail addresses (separated by commas).
`datetime`	It expects a date and time with UTC time zone.
`date`	It expects a date.
`month`	It expects a date with a year and a month, but no time zone.
`week`	It expects a date that consists of a week-year number and a week number.
`time`	It expects a time-value such as hours, minutes, seconds, and fractional seconds.
`datetime-local`	It expects date and time with no time zone.
`number`	It expects numerical input.
`range`	It expects a numerical input and displays a slider.
`color`	It expects color value and displays a color palette to choose from.

Along with the addition to the `<input>` types, new features have been added to the already existing ones such as the File input element, which now supports multifile selection using the `multiple` attribute. The **browse** button will display the file dialog and then you can select files from your local disk or `SkyDrive`; the files can be sent to the server as part of the form data when the form is submitted.

You can also take advantage of the `progress` element that represents the progress of a task, as specified by the W3C. It can be used to show the progress of a large file being uploaded or a media resource that is being loaded. The progress of a task is determined by two attributes of this element:

- The `value` attribute, which indicates how much progress has been made
- The `max` attribute, which indicates the total amount of work required till task completion

The following code uses a `progress` element and a button, and the script adds the value specified in the JavaScript function parameter to its existing value. When you load the sample and try it, you will see the progress bar visually updating the completion progress.

The following is the HTML code:

```
<button id="clickBtn" onclick="updateProgress(10)">Update Progress</button>
  Progress: <progress id="prog" max="100"></progress>
```

The following is the JavaScript code:

```
<script>
//get the progress element and add the value to it with every click
var progressBar = document.getElementById('prog');
function updateProgress(newValue){
progressBar.value = progressBar.value + newValue;
}
</script>
```

Easy validation

HTML5's new `<input>` types along with the validation attributes such as `required` and `pattern`, and the pseudo CSS3 selectors allow browser-based validation, where you can catch a form's input errors without a single line of code or script. This was previously impossible and needed a custom JavaScript code or a JavaScript library. Basically, it provides client-side form validation without JavaScript.

We'll start with the most trivial validation, filling a required field. In order to achieve this, we need to add the `required` attribute to an `<input>` element.

The `required` attribute can be set on the `<input>` elements with type `text`, `URL`, `email`, `checkbox`, or `radio`, and on `select` and `textarea` elements. It is a Boolean attribute and can only be set on an element.

We specify that filling a value for a field is mandatory by simply adding the `required` attribute. In the following code listing, you will find a couple of `<input>` elements with the `required` attribute:

```
<form action="/" method="post">
  <label>Checkbox:</label>
    <input type="checkbox" required />
  <label>Radio:</label>
```

```
      <select>
        ...
      </select>
    <label>Text:</label>
      <input type="search" required />
    <label>Range:</label>
      <input type="range" min="5" max="10" step="5" />
    <label>URL:</label>
      <input type="url"  required />
    <label>File:</label>
      <input type="file" accept=".mp3" />
      <input type="submit" name="submit" value=" Submit " />
  </form>
```

Once the `required` attribute is added, and then when you click on the **submit** button, all the fields in the form will be validated; an error is returned if any of the fields are incorrect. The required fields are highlighted, and moreover, default messages are provided to notify the user that these fields are required in the form.

You can see the following screenshot displaying the output of the preceding code:

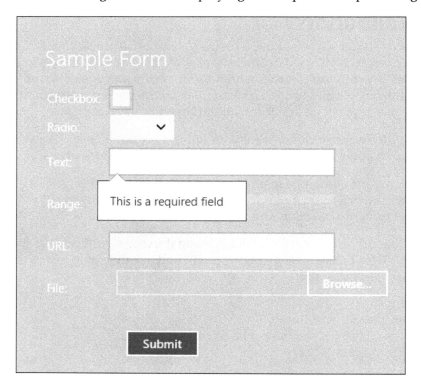

We can apply one or more styles using the CSS3 pseudo-selector `required` (more on that in the next chapter). For example, the following style adds a CSS3 pseudo-class `required`, which will look for all the `input` elements in the document that have the `required` attribute, and style it with the `yellow` `border-color`.

```
input:required {
  border-color: Yellow;
}
```

If you want to apply a style that affects all the non-required elements in the form, well that's very easy; just add the `optional` pseudo-class and give it a style just as we did with the `required` class. In the following code, we apply a `LightGray` `border-color` to all the `input` elements that don't have a `required` attribute.

```
input:optional {
  border-color: LightGray;
}
```

HTML5 forms not only validate for required fields, but they also check the content of the field values and validate it either automatically, as in the URL and `email` input types, or by using the `pattern` attribute. The `pattern` attribute uses a regular expression to define the valid format that the element value must match, for example, a telephone number or social security number.

The following example shows the syntax for a `password` field, which is both required and must have a valid input with a minimum length of eight characters. And here, the default validation message is replaced by the text provided in the `title` attribute:

```
<input type="password" required pattern="[^\s]{8}[^\s]*"
title="Passwords must be at least 8 characters long."/>
```

There are more attributes that add to the validation technique, such as `placeholder`, which provides the users with a hint message displayed in light text until the user starts typing inside the element; the hint could be about the value they should enter in the field. For example, you can add a demo e-mail address in the `email` field such as:

```
<input type="email" placeholder="email@example.com" />
```

You can check for the maximum number of characters allowed in a `text` or a `textarea` input using the `maxlength` attribute. Also, we have the `min`, `max`, and `step` attributes used with the `range` element to validate the values entered for that element. The `min` and `max` attributes check for the minimum and maximum values that can be entered, while the `step` attribute checks for the allowed values.

You can also specify acceptable file MIME types with the `accept` attribute. As you may have noticed in the preceding code listing, the `accept` attribute was added to the `<input type="file" />` element, which is the only element to be used with it. Once you add this to the file control, and then when you try to browse for a file using Windows 8 File Explorer, only the types that are in the `accept` list will be displayed.

HTML5 form validation is the default behavior; no code is needed to activate it, but you can turn it off by adding the `formnovalidate` attribute to the **submit** button or any `<input>` element. This attribute allows a form to be submitted without being validated.

Assigning custom data attributes

With HTML5, we now have the ability to assign custom data attributes to any HTML5 element. The W3C defines it as:

Attribute that is intended to store custom data private to the page or application, for which there are no more appropriate attributes or elements.

These new custom data attributes consist of two parts:

- **Attribute name**: It must start with the prefix data- and should be followed with at least one character and should not contain uppercase characters
- **Attribute value**: It must be a string value

Let's add a custom attribute to a `<div>` tag as shown in the following code:

```
<div id="bookList" data-category="TechnicalBooks">
Developing for windows 8
</div>
```

You can see the custom attribute name `data-category` and the attribute value `TechnicalBooks` assigned to the `<div>` element. This data can be retrieved and updated by your JavaScript code using the native `getAttribute` and `setAttribute` methods, because the custom data attributes are considered to be part of the page on which they are used. The following is the code sample that shows how to manipulate the custom attributes using native JavaScript:

```
function getSetCategory() {
  var bookList = document.getElementById("bookList");
//get the value of the attribute
  var bookCategory = bookList.getAttribute('data-category');
//set the value for the attribute
```

```
  bookList.setAttribute('data-category', 'HealthBooks');
//remove the attribute
  bookList.removeAttribute('data-category');
}
```

The HTML5 specification clearly states that the data attributes should not be used to replace an existing attribute or an element that may be more semantically appropriate. For example, it would be inappropriate to add a data-time attribute to specify a time value in a span element as the following code shows:

```
<span data-time="08:00">8am<span>
```

The most appropriate and more semantic element to use would be a time element, as the following code shows:

```
<time datetime="08:00">8am</time>
```

When developing Windows 8 apps, we can use the Windows library for JavaScript (WinJS) to achieve more advanced binding of data to HTML elements. The Win8 JavaScript library utilizes the HTML data-* attributes to provide an easy way to programmatically implement data binding.

Summary

In HTML5, there are new semantically rich elements that can convey the purpose of their use. There are media elements that allow you to easily add audio and video to your application, and new input types and attributes that you can use to create intelligent and interactive forms and bind them to data on-the-fly, all with less markup and code than ever before.

In the next chapter, we will have a look at the new and rich CSS3 features available for us when developing for Windows 8, and how we can use them to style and apply layouts to our HTML.

2
Styling with CSS3

HTML defines the document/page structure and lists the elements it contains. But the job of defining the layout, the positioning, and the styling of those elements is the sole responsibility of CSS. **A cascading style sheet (CSS)**, as the name suggests, is basically a sheet that contains a list of style rules. Each CSS style rule links a **selector**, which defines what is going to be styled, to a declaration block, which includes a single or a set of styles, which in turn define the effect(s) you want applied to that associated selector. The syntax of a basic style rule would look like this

```
selector { property: value; property: value; }
```

Throughout this chapter, we will go over the following topics: CSS3 selectors, Grid and Flexbox, Animation and Transforms, and Media Queries. These topics cover some of the CSS3 features that are frequently used when developing a Windows Store app with JavaScript.

The power of CSS3 selectors

CSS selectors are very powerful and come in handy when formatting an HTML document. Using selectors is sometimes tricky, as selecting exactly what you want, and then ensuring that the style rules applied are affecting just the elements that you intended, is a tedious mission. But when done properly with the right selectors, the outcome is very rewarding. Mastering the use of selectors will result in a less complex CSS, minimizing the probability of having redundant styles and over-defining the HTML with classes and IDs, thus ensuring a better performance. The selector can simply be an HTML element, a class, an element ID, or it can even be the element's position in the DOM.

The following is a list of CSS selectors; we will start with the basics and get to the new selectors introduced in CSS3:

- **The asterisk (*) symbol**: This is the `catch-all` selector, called the universal type selector, and is used to target every element in the document. It is often used with CSS Reset to reset all the default styles.

  ```
  * { margin: 0; }
  ```

- **The HTML element**: It is called the type selector and is used to select all the elements in the document according to their type. For example, the following selector will target every `<p>` element in the DOM, change the color of the text to red, and underline it.

  ```
  p { color: red; text-decoration: underline; }
  ```

   Using the `<body>` element as a selector will target the document's body, thereby selecting every element as if you are using the asterisk (*).

- **The ID selector**: It is specified by the value in the id attribute of the element prefixed with the hash (#) symbol. The ID should be the element's name and, more importantly, it must be unique. The name should be a clear reference to the element. For instance, it would be quite clear to have an `id` value of `mainMenu` for a `nav` element. For example:

  ```
  <nav id="mainMenu"></nav>
  ```

  Moreover, being unique means that logically there should be no other element with an `id` value of `mainMenu` on the page. Since the `id` should always be unique, the selector will target only one element in the HTML document. For example, if you have a `<div>` element with an `id` value of `logo` as follows:

  ```
  <div id="logo"></div>
  ```

  Then the corresponding selector will be:

  ```
  #logo { float: left; width: 200px; }
  ```

- **The class selector**: It is specified by the name of a class prefixed with a period (.) and targets all the elements with the matching class name. The basic syntax for this selector is as follows:

  ```
  .highlighted { font-weight: bold; background-color:
    yellow; }
  ```

Any element with this class name will have bold text in a yellow background color. Classes should be applied when you want to style more than one element, specifically, a set of elements that have something in common. Bear in mind that contrary to the id property, the class name can never be used to uniquely identify an element. Moreover, the class property may have more than a single value; similarly, the same class may apply to more than one element. Although the use of class selectors may seem general, you can use it in a more specific manner by prefixing it with a type selector. For example, the following code snippet will target only the <div> elements that have the class **highlighted**:

```
div.highlighted { font-weight: bold; background-color: yellow; }
```

Also, you can chain class selectors to target all the elements that have all of the specified classes.

Attribute selectors

The attribute selector is used to select elements based on their attributes. It checks whether an attribute is present; if yes, it checks the value of the attribute. The attribute should be enclosed within square braces. If the square braces contain only the name of the attribute, it will check if the attribute exists on the element. That's why it's also called the existence selector. In the following code snippet, the selector will target only the anchor elements having the title attribute:

```
a[title] { text-decoration: none; color: #000; }
```

The preceding syntax is helpful when checking for attributes that do not hold a value. If you remember, in the previous chapter we mentioned that some attributes do not need a value, such as the required attribute with the <input> elements, or the loop attribute with the audio and video elements. The following selector will look for all the audio elements that have the loop attribute and hide it:

```
audio[loop] { display: none; }
```

To target the element(s) that exactly matches the specified attribute value, we will use the equality attribute marked with an equal symbol (=) and the value wrapped within quotes. So, if we want to target all input elements that have the value email in their type attribute, the syntax will look like the following:

```
input[type="email"] { text-decoration: none; color: #000; }
```

Also, under the attribute selector category, we have the **prefix** or the "starts with" attribute selector, which is used to check if an attribute has a value that starts with some value. The following syntax will match all the images that have an `id` value starting with `home`. For example, if you want to target all the images in your home page, you can add `home` to the `id`, thus having `homeLogo`, `homeBanner`, and so on, and apply a margin of 10 px to it:

```
img[id^='home'] { margin:10px; }
```

Similarly, we have the **suffix** selector or the "ends with" attribute selector, which will select all the elements whose attribute ends with the value you specify. The suffix selector is marked with the dollar ($) symbol before the equal (=) sign, and the syntax will look as follows:

```
a[href$=".jpg"] { color: red; }
```

This will target all the anchor elements whose `href` attribute holds a value that ends with `.jpg`.

Another attribute selector is the **substring** selector, also known as the "contains" selector. As the name suggests, it matches the attribute value containing the value specified in the selector. It is marked with the asterisk (*) symbol before the equal (=) sign, and the syntax will look as follows:

```
ul[id*="Nav"] { float: left; list-style-type: none; }
```

The preceding syntax will match all the `<ul>` elements that have an ID containing the string `Nav`. For example, you have multiple `<ul>` elements used for navigational purposes and marked with IDs such as `secondaryNav`, `sidebarNav`, and so on.

Also, we have the **hyphen** selector, marked with `|=`, which is used to match all the attribute values that are exactly equal and is immediately followed by a hyphen. You might use this selector rarely but a typical use for it would be with values that include a hyphen, for example, the `lang` attribute. The following listing will target all the elements with a value that exactly matches "en", additionally followed by a hyphen, and will return `en`, `en-us`, `en-uk`, and so on:

```
ul[lang|="en"] { display: none; }
```

The last attribute selector would be the **whitespace** selector, which targets the specified attribute value that exactly matches in a space-delimited list of values. In the following code snippet, we have a `<p>` element with a custom `data-` attribute, containing three space-separated values, named `new events local`, and the selector will match this element since its `data-post-type` value matches exactly the value specified as `events`.

The following is the HTML code:

```
<p data-post-type="new events local"></p>
```

And the CSS code is as follows:

```
p[data-post-type~="events"] { float: left; color: red }
```

 Note that, with HTML5, any attribute starting with `data-` is valid, unlike its predecessor that considers only the recognized attributes as valid.

Combinator selectors

A CSS selector can contain multiple selectors, that is, a combination of simple selectors. A combinator selector contains more than one simple selector joined by a combinator. The combinator is a symbol that represents the relationship between the selectors. We already had three different combinators in CSS2, and CSS3 added one extra. Listed as follows are the four selectors, the combinators used, and what each selector matches:

Selector	Combinator	Target
Descendant	Space Character	Matches the elements that are descendants of the specified element.
Direct Descendant (Child Selector)	>	Matches the elements that are a direct descendant of the specified element.
Adjacent Sibling	+	Matches the elements that are an adjacent sibling (immediately following) to the specified element.
General Sibling	~	Matches the elements that are an adjacent sibling to the specified element.

The preceding selectors are described as follows:

- **The Descendant selector**: It is marked by a space character as a combinator and it will select all elements that are descendants of a specified element. It is as if we are applying an additional filter on the first simple selector. The first selector represents the parent element, and the second is the child (descendant) element you are trying to match. For example, the following code snippet will match all the anchor elements that have the `<li>` element as their parent:

The HTML code is as follows:

```
<ul>
    <li><a href="#">Item 1</a></li>
    <li><a href="#">Item 2</a></li>
    <li><a href="#">Item 3</a></li>
</ul>
```

The CSS selector is as follows:

```
li a { text-decoration: none; color: #000; }
```

- **The Direct Descendant selector**: It is marked by the greater-than (>) sign as a combinator and has the basic form E>F, which matches every F element that is a direct descendant (child) of the E element. In the following code snippet, only the <p> elements that are immediate children of the <div> element are going to be colored blue while the rest are not.

  The HTML code is as follows:

```
<div>
    <p>some content inside a div</p>
</div>
<p> standalone content …</p>
<div>
    <p> contentinside a div </p>
</div>
<header>
    <p> content inside a header </p>
</header>
```

  The CSS code is as follows:

```
div > p { color: Blue; }
```

- **The Adjacent Sibling selector**: It is marked by a plus (+) sign as a combinator, and matches all the sibling elements that are immediately following the parent element. So, there can be no elements in between the sibling elements. If it is a bit complex, the following example will explain it. The selector will apply red color only to one <p> element.

  The HTML code is as follows:

```
<h1>Heading</h1>
<p>This p element is a sibling and adjacent to the h1
</p>
<p>This p element is a sibling but not adjacent to the h1
</p>
```

The CSS code is as follows:

```
h1 + p { color: Red; }
```

- **The General Sibling selector**: It is marked by the tilde (~) sign as a combinator, and is a new addition in CSS3. It is used to select all the elements that are siblings of a given element. So, if we apply the selector to the HTML in the preceding example, both the <p> elements will match and will be colored red, as they are both siblings of h1.

```
h1 ~ p { color: Red; }
```

Pseudo-class selectors

A pseudo-class is similar to a class but, since it is in-built, you do not have to explicitly add it in the HTML code. Also, it differs in syntax; a class selector is preceded by a period (.), whereas a pseudo-class is preceded by a colon (:). In its basic form, a pseudo-class selector will take the following form:

```
selector:pseudo-class { property: value }
```

You can specify a pseudo-class without a selector, and it will invoke the default type selector. So, if we specify :hover alone, it will match all the elements and apply the style rule to anything in the document that can be hovered on. Else, you can be more detailed and apply the pseudo-class selector to a specific HTML element. For example, the following code snippet will apply a pink color on all the <p> elements when hovered over:

```
p:hover { color: pink; }
```

Pseudo-classes existed in CSS prior to CSS3 and you are most probably familiar with the famous :hover, :visited, and :active pseudo-classes that represent the different states of the anchor element. CSS3 introduced many more powerful pseudo-classes such as :required, :valid, :nth-child(n), :first-child, :last-child, :only-child, :first-of-type, :last-of-type, and several others.

Pseudo-element selectors

Pseudo-elements represent parts of elements, such as the first line of a paragraph, or the part that appears after an element. Similar to a pseudo-class that acts as a class, a pseudo-element behaves as an element but is in-built and does not need to be defined in the HTML code. Pseudo-elements are distinguished by a double colon (::), which was introduced in CSS3. Note that all the pseudo-elements that were introduced before CSS3 used a single colon (:), similar to the pseudo-class syntax.

The following code snippet will select all the generated content defined by the `content` style property that appears after the `<p>` element:

The HTML code is as follows:

```
<p>Paragraph content goes here</p>
```

The CSS code is as follows:

```
p::after {
    content: " 'I come after a paragraph' ";
    color: blue; background-color: yellow;
}
```

The output will be:

Paragraph content goes here 'I come after a paragraph'

The following table lists the pseudo-elements:

::first-letter	Matches the first letter in an element.
::first-line	Selects the first line in an element.
::before	Selects the content generated before an element.
::after	Selects the content generated after an element.
::selection	Selects any content that the user might have highlighted, including text within an editable text field, such as input type text, or any element with the `contenteditable` attribute declared.

Although you can have the same behavior programmatically by adding classes to your HTML code using JavaScript, it is easier to add pseudo-classes and pseudo-elements to your selectors; moreover, it gives you cleaner code.

Creating fluid layouts with Grid and Flexbox

When it comes to implementing the design principles set by Microsoft to build attractive, intuitive, and interactive Windows 8 apps, layout is very important. It is common to define a page layout using HTML structural elements such as `<div>` and `<table>`, and the positioning style rules.

But now, there is a more flexible way to do it with the CSS3 advanced layout features, namely **Grid** layout and **Flexbox** (**Flexible box**) layout. These layout systems allow you to easily implement an adaptive and fluid layout.

The Grid layout

It offers a very simple way to create fluid and adaptable layouts for a Windows 8 app. It is ideal for implementing a full screen UI since the grid can automatically expand to fill in all the space that is available. The Grid layout allows you to align and position its child elements as columns and rows, entirely using CSS, and is independent of their order in the HTML code. It enables more fluidity in layouts than what would be possible with the approach that uses floats or scripts.

The following example demonstrates how we traditionally used floats to position elements:

The HTML code is as follows:

```
<div class="container">
  <div class="leftDiv"></div>
  <div class="rightDiv"></div>
</div>
```

The CSS code is as follows:

```
.container { width: 200px; height:50px; border: 1px solid black; }
.leftDiv { float:left; width: 100px; height:50px;
  background-color:blue}
.rightDiv { float:right; width: 50px; height:50px;
  background-color:red}
```

The preceding code will result in the following multicolor box. The container has a black border surrounding the two divs inside, the blue div to the left and the red one to the right, and the white space in between is the remaining unoccupied space:

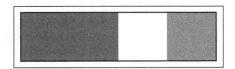

The Grid layout is specified by setting the `display` style rule property of an element to `-ms-grid`, or you can use the `-ms-inline-grid` property for an inline-level grid element. You may have noticed the vendor prefix `-ms`(Microsoft-specific), which is because the status of this CSS feature is still a Working Draft; adding this vendor prefix allows it to work with both Internet Explorer 10 and Windows Store apps using JavaScript in Windows 8. The following is an example:

```
.divGrid {
  display: -ms-grid;
  -ms-grid-columns: 120px 1fr;
  -ms-grid-rows: 120px 1fr;
}
.column1row1 {
  -ms-grid-column: 1;
  -ms-grid-row: 1;
}
.column2row1 {
  -ms-grid-column: 2;
  -ms-grid-row: 1;
}
```

The `display: -ms-grid;` property creates a grid; afterwards, we define the columns and rows and specify their sizes using the following properties: `-ms-grid-column` and `-ms-grid-rows`. The `-ms-grid-columns` property specifies the width of each column, and `-ms-grid-rows` specifies the height of each row, in that grid. The width and height values in these two properties respectively are separated by a space character. In the preceding example, the `-ms-grid-columns: 120px 1fr;` property creates two columns; the first one has a width of 120 px and the second one has a width value of 1 fr, that is, one fractional unit, which means that the width of the second column will automatically fill in all of the remaining available space. The same concept applies for rows. The remaining two classes in the preceding code snippet will position the elements in these classes into columns and rows of the grid using the `-ms-grid-column` and `-ms-grid-row` properties.

The **fraction units (fr)** designate how the available space should be divided among the columns or rows according to their fractional values. For example, if we have a four-columns layout such as the following: `-ms-grid-columns: 100px 100px 1fr 2fr;`, column 3 takes one fraction and column 4 takes two fractions of the total remaining space. Hence, the total remaining space is now 3 fr; column 3 is set to 1 fr divided by the total (3), so both one-third of the remaining space and column 4 having 2 fr will be assigned two-thirds of the remaining space.

In the preceding example, we used px and fr units to specify the size of the columns and rows. Additionally, we can do so using standard length units (such as px or em), or the percentage of the element's width or height. Also, we can use the following keywords:

- auto: This keyword makes the size of the column or row stretch to fit the content inside
- min-content: This keyword sets the size of the column or row to the minimum size of any child element
- max-content: This keyword sets the size of the column or row to the maximum size of any child element
- minmax(a,b): This keyword sets the size of the column or row to a value between a and b as much as the available space allows

The following table lists the properties associated with the Grid layout:

-ms-grid-column	Specifies in which column of the grid the element will reside. The numbering system is of the **1-based index** type.
-ms-grid-columns	Specifies a width value for each of the grid columns.
-ms-grid-column-span	Specifies the number of columns that the element will occupy in the grid.
-ms-grid-column-align	Specifies a value for the horizontal alignment of the element inside the column.
-ms-grid-row	Specifies in which row of the grid the element will reside. The numbering system is of the 1-based index type.
-ms-grid-rows	Specifies a height value for each of the grid rows.
-ms-grid-row-span	Specifies the number of rows that the element will occupy in the grid.
-ms-grid-row-align	Specifies a value for the vertical alignment of the element inside the row.

Moreover, the Grid layout exposes a rich set of properties that allows you to easily cater to the changes in the view states and orientation of the app. We will discuss that later on when we get to the design of the app.

The Flexbox layout

The second layout model we have is the Flexbox mode, another recent addition in CSS3. Similar to the Grid layout, the Flexbox layout is enabled using the display property and also requires a Microsoft-specific vendor prefix as it is still a **World Wide Web Consortium (W3C)** Working Draft. The Flexbox layout is used to make the relative position and the size of elements stay constant, even if the window sizes of the screen and browser change. Compared to floats, Flexbox provides a better and easier control on the position and size of elements. The advantage you have with Flexbox layout is that it enables relative positioning and dimensions of the elements inside it, since it considers the available space. This allows you to create a fluid layout that maintains the position and size of the elements relative to each other; hence, it enables the elements inside a Flexbox container to resize and reposition themselves when the dimensions of the browser or app window change. A Flexbox layout would be ideal for building apps that present any digital print media, such as a newspaper or a magazine.

As with the Grid layout, it is quite easy to create a container with a Flexbox layout by setting the display property to -ms-flexbox. After creating a Flexbox container, we can start manipulating the elements inside it, using the following properties:

- -ms-flex-direction: It specifies the orientation of the child elements using the following keyword values: row (initial value), column, row-reverse, and column-reverse. We will go over each one of the values, and show the effect it applies, in the following example. And what better way to explain it than actual code? So,o suppose we have the following HTML and CSS code snippets:

```
<div class="flexit">
  <div>1</div>
  <div>2</div>
  <div>3</div>
</div>

.flexit {
  width:160px;
  height:100px;
  border:2px solid brown;
  display:-ms-flexbox;
  -ms-flex-direction: row;
}
.flexit div {
  background-color:red;
  width:50px;
```

```
    height:25px;
    text-align:center;
    color:white;
}
.flexit div:first-child {
    background-color:green;
    height:30px;
}
.flexit div:last-child {
    background-color:blue;
    height:30px;
}
```

The preceding syntax creates a Flexbox container with the `flexit` class that wraps in a Flexbox layout the child `<div>` elements marked with text 1, 2, and 3 for tracking. We apply some styles and background colors to mark the child elements.

So the following values in the `-ms-flex-direction` property will give us the results in the following table. Notice how the order and the positioning of the elements change without adding anything to the markup:

Property	The Flexbox container	The order and the positioning of the elements
row		The child elements are positioned from left to right, in the same order of appearance in the HTML markup.
row-reverse		The child elements are positioned from right to left, in the reverse order of appearance in the HTML markup.

| column | | The child elements are positioned from top to bottom, in the same order of appearance in the HTML markup from left to right. |
| column-reverse | | The child elements are positioned from bottom to top, in the same order of appearance in the HTML markup. |

- `-ms-flex-align`: This property specifies the alignment of the child elements in a Flexbox container. It takes the following keyword values: `start`, `end`, `center`, `stretch`, and `baseline`. The alignment is always perpendicular to the layout axis defined in the `-ms-flex-direction` property; so, if the orientation is horizontal, it will set the alignment to vertical and vice versa. For example, if the orientation is `row` (horizontal), the value `start` will set the alignment to top (vertical).

- `-ms-flex-pack`: This property specifies how the available space is divided between the child elements of the Flexbox container, parallel to the axis defined by the `-ms-flex-direction` property, unlike the alignment property described earlier. It takes the following keyword values: `start`, `end`, `center`, and `justify`.

- `-ms-flex-wrap`: This property enables the child elements to overflow and wrap to the next line or columns, and specifies the direction of that flow. It takes the following keyword values: `none`, `wrap`, and `wrap-reverse`.

CSS-powered animations

CSS transforms allow you to manipulate HTML elements in a way that previously was only possible with scripts. It enables rotation, translation, scaling, and skewing of elements, and enables the transformation of elements in 2D and 3D. CSS animations enable you to smoothly change the style properties over a period of time, allowing you to design complex animations with better rendering performance when compared to JavaScript-powered animations. Working with the two combined, you can do magic on your app.

CSS3 animations

CSS3 revolutionized animation in web development. Earlier, creating animations required animated images, plugins such as Flash, or some heavy scripting. Although jQuery and other supporting libraries made it a bit easier for developers to create animations with JavaScript, still it cannot compete with the performance capability that the CSS animations offer. Basically, an animation defines an effect that allows an element to change one or many styles, such as color, size, position, opacity, and others, within a time frame. Also, with CSS3 animations, you can allow multiple intermediate changes in styles during the animation itself, other than the ones specified at the beginning and end of the animation.

In order to create an animation, you will need the @keyframe CSS rule, which is used to specify the styles that will be changed during the animation. The following is the code snippet that creates a @keyframe rule named demo and changes the background color from red to yellow, and halfway through, at 50percent, it changes the opacity to zero:

```
@keyframes demo {
    from { background: red;    }
    50% { opacity: 0;          }
    to { background: yellow; }
}
```

Afterwards, we bind the animation that is defined in the @keyframe rule to the element (or the selector) we want the effect applied to. Left alone without being attached to any element, the animation will not be applied anywhere. We will need to specify at least two animation properties when binding the animation to a selector:

- Name
- Duration

For example:

```
#logo { animation: demo 4s }
```

The preceding example binds the animation named demo that we created using the @keyframe rule, with a duration of 4 seconds, to the element with ID #logo.

Animations are triggered automatically as soon as they are defined in the DOM. You can specify a certain delay time to avoid that, or you can trigger the animation by code. The animation has six major properties as shown below:

```
div {
    animation-name: demo;
```

```
    animation-duration: 3s;
    animation-timing-function: ease-in;
    animation-delay: 3s;
    animation-iteration-count: 2;
    animation-direction: normal;
}
```

Or we can use the animation shorthand property by which we can combine all of these properties into a single line:

```
div { animation: demo 3s ease-in 3s 2 normal; }
```

Developers are still a bit hesitant to use CSS3 animations, or any other HTML5 feature for that matter, due to browser support. In order to address this problem of browser compatibility, some style rules had to be defined with vendor-prefixes. For example, an animation definition would be duplicated to support other browsers, each with its own vendor prefixes as follows:

```
-webkit-animation: 5s linear 2s infinite alternate;
-moz-animation: 5s linear 2s infinite alternate;
-o-animation: 5s linear 2s infinite alternate;
animation: 5s linear 2s infinite alternate;
```

But when developing for Windows 8, you can reduce it to one, which is the standard. Worrying about multi-browser support is the least of your concerns as Windows 8 supports all the standards that work for Internet Explorer 10.

CSS3 transforms

Another advantage of CSS3 is the concept of 2D and 3D transforms, which enables you to manipulate the elements in your app in a way that was not possible using CSS. It enables you to create rotation, scaling, skewing, and translation of HTML elements in 2D and, newly, in 3D space without the need for a plugin or scripts, defined by the W3C under the **CSS transforms** specification.

Transforms are created using the `transform` property, which holds a list of transform functions to be applied to the specified element. The property value can be set to one or more (space-delimited) transform functions, which will be applied in the order they are listed. Following is a sample code of the `transform` property that applies the rotate function:

```
div { transform: rotate(90deg) translateX(100px); }
```

The result of the preceding `transform` property is that the element is rotated 90 degrees and then translated (moved) 100 px horizontally to the right.

The list of functions available for the `transform` property includes `matrix()`, `matrix3d()`, `perspective()`, `rotate()`, `rotate3d()`, `rotateX()`, `rotateY()`, `rotateZ()`, `scale()`, `scale3d()`, `scaleX()`, `scaleY()`, `scaleZ()`, `skew()`, `skewX()`, `skewY()`, `translate()`, `translate3d()`, `translateX()`, `translateY()`, and `translateZ()`. These functions are provided with the CSS3 IntelliSense features in Visual Studio; thus, when writing a `transform` property, you will be prompted to choose one of those functions.

> Visual Studio 2012 has enhanced support for CSS with features such as Regions, IntelliSense, vendor prefixes, and built-in snippets, thereby making it very easy and convenient to develop apps for Windows 8 using HTML5 and CSS.

Introducing media queries

Your Windows 8 app should have a fluid and responsive UI, as the same app will be downloaded and opened either on a tablet, a PC with a large monitor, or a phone. Your app should adapt to the different view states (full screen portrait or landscape, filled or snapped) and display accordingly. It should look good and function well when the users flip the screen between portrait and landscape, when they zoom, when they snap the app, and so on. Too much stuff to look out for, you might say? Worry not, because if you are developing using a JavaScript app, the answer to all your concerns is **CSS Media Queries**!

By using CSS media queries, you can manage the changes to the layout by easily defining different styles to apply to the HTML elements in your app, depending on the view state and size of the current media. You can use a separate media query to tailor for each view state, or you can combine media queries to apply the same set of styles to multiple view states. The basic syntax of a media query is as follows:

```
@media MediaType TargetMediaProperty{MediaRule}
```

It is a logical expression that is either `true` or `false`, and consists of the following:

- **@media**: It is a keyword that indicates a media query
- **MediaType**: It is used to specify the type of media we are targeting; it can have one of the following values: `screen` for computer screens, `print` for documents viewed in print mode, and `all` for all devices
- **TargetMediaProperty**: It is used to create more specific queries by adding conditions such as orientation and size
- **MediaRule**: It is used to specify one or more style rules that will be applied in case the media query is evaluated to `true`

A simple example would look like the following:

```
@media screen and (max-width: 1024px) {
  body {
    background-color: orange;
  }
}
```

The preceding media query will check whether the medium is a screen and the width of window does not exceed 400 pixels. If `true`, it will apply the orange background color to the body element.

The following code snippet checks for the orientation:

```
@media all and (orientation: portrait) {
  ...
}
```

We can also include the Microsoft-specific vendor property `-ms-view-state` to check for different view states that the app can handle. For example:

```
@media all and (-ms-view-state: snapped) {
  ...
}
```

Summary

In this chapter, we tried to cover and learn as much as possible from the new and rich CSS3 features and describe which ones are available for us when developing apps for Windows 8. We looked in detail at the CSS selectors and learned to use them to filter the DOM elements according to our need. We learned about new layout techniques using the Grid and Flexbox display properties.

We saw what magic we can do with the animation and transform properties, and got to have a look at the power of media queries to help us build a responsive layout. In short, CSS3 is a wonderland and you will need to get familiar with its features in order to harness all its powers.

In the next chapter, we will go over the main features provided by the Windows Library for JavaScript, which is the backbone of the Windows Store app that is built using JavaScript.

3
JavaScript for Windows Apps

In this chapter, we will get introduced to some of the features provided by the **Windows Library for JavaScript** (the `WinJS` library) that has been introduced by Microsoft to provide access to Windows Runtime for the Windows Store apps using JavaScript. Windows Library for JavaScript is a library of CSS and JavaScript files. It contains a set of powerful and feature-rich JavaScript objects, functions, and methods organized into namespaces, with the aim of making it easier for developers to create Windows Store apps using JavaScript.

We will also learn about asynchronous programming with `WinJS` and see how we can query the document for elements and manipulate these elements using the functions provided by the `WinJS.Utilities` namespace. Next we will learn about the `xhr` function and its use and finally get introduced to the set of UI controls provided by the Windows Library for JavaScript.

Asynchronous programming with Promise objects

When building a Windows 8 app, the stress is on having a responsive UI, which is one of the main characteristics of a Windows 8 Store app. In *Chapter 2*, *Styling with CSS3*, we got to see how we can achieve that at the styling level. The responsive UI also includes having a responsive functionality whereby the code running behind the scenes not only blocks the app's UI all of a sudden but also makes it unresponsive to any user input while some logic or functionality executes.

JavaScript, as a programming language, is single-threaded, which means that a synchronous execution of a long-running process will block all other executions until that process has completed. Thus, you should avoid synchronous execution whenever you can. The solution to this predicament is asynchronous processing, which is essential to create responsive, high-performance apps. One way of achieving asynchronous processing is by using the **callback function mechanism**. A callback function is used as a hook point for continuing the processing after a previous asynchronous operation has terminated. A typical example is a call to a server-side backend.

```
//code sample using jQuery
function longRunningComputation(callbackFunc){
    setTimeout(function(){
        //computation
        //once finished, invoke the callback with the result
        callbackFunc(computationResult);
    }, 1000);
}
```

This function is then invoked as follows:

```
longRunningComputation(function(compResult) {
    //do something meaningful with the result

});
```

The callback functions are the typical solution to asynchronous calls but they have a drawback: they create deep chains, especially when you place multiple asynchronous operations in a chain where subsequent functions rely on the result of the previous computation. Windows Library for JavaScript along with Windows Runtime provides a more elegant solution using a mechanism called **Promise**, which simplifies asynchronous programming. Promise, as the name suggests, indicates that something will happen in the future and the Promise is said to be fulfilled after that something has completed.

In the following code sample, we create a function called sumAsync that will return a WinJS.Promise object and will execute asynchronously when we call it in the clickMe() function:

```
function clickMe() {
    sumAsync().then(
        function complete(result) {
```

```
                document.getElementById("result").textContent = "The
promise has completed, with the result: " + result;
        },
        function error(result) {
                document.getElementById("result").innerHTML = "An Error
has occurred </br>" + result;
        },
        function progress(result) {
                document.getElementById("result").innerHTML += "The
promise is in progress, hold on please." + result;
        })
}
function sumAsync() {
    return new WinJS.Promise(function (comp, err, prog) {
        setTimeout(function () {
            try {
                var sum = 3 + 4;
                var i;
                for (i = 1; i < 100; i++) {
                    prog(i);
                }
                comp(sum);
            } catch (e) {
                err(e);
            }
        }, 1000);
    });
}
```

We can deduce from the preceding code sample that, Promise is basically an object. This object implements a method named then, which in turn takes the following three functions as parameters:

- A function that will be called when the Promise object completes and has been fulfilled successfully

- A function that will be called when an error arises while the Promise object is being fulfilled, known as future

- A function that will be called while Promise is being fulfilled, to indicate the progress information, known as deferred

In Visual Studio, when you add a `then` method to a function, you will be prompted in the IntelliSense pop-up window to enter these parameters, as shown in the following screenshot:

```
sumAsync().then(|
              WinJS.Promise then(Function onComplete, [Function onError], [Function onProgress])
```

You can use the `then` method with any function that returns `Promise`; since it returns `Promise`, you can chain multiple `then` functions. For example:

```
sumAsync()
    .then(function () { return XAsync(); })
    .then(function () { return YAsync(); })
    .done(function () {  endProcessing();})
```

In the previous example, we appended multiple `then` methods to the functions and completed the processing with the `done` method.

 The `done` method takes the same parameter as `then`. However, the difference between the two is that `done` returns `undefined` instead of `Promise`, so you cannot chain it. In addition, the `done` method throws an exception if an `error` function is not provided to handle any errors that occur during processing, while the `then` function does not throw an exception and instead returns the `Promise` object in the `error` state.

All the Windows Runtime APIs that are exposed to Windows Store apps are wrapped in `Promise` objects, exposing methods and functions that return a `Promise` object, allowing you to easily implement asynchronous processes in your app.

Querying the DOM with WinJS.Utilities

The UI of the app is described in HTML and the corresponding styles. When the app is launched, you should expect different user interactions with the UI. The user will touch some sections of your app; he/she will scroll, zoom in and out, or add or remove items. Moreover, the app might interact with the user through dialogs or conversations and through posting notifications on the screen. Responding to such interactions is handled by code and in our case, specifically by JavaScript code. That's where `WinJS.Utilities` comes in handy, by providing helper functions to do that; for example, functions to add/remove CSS classes or to insert HTML elements. But before anything interacts with the user, you have to select the function using JavaScript, which is called **querying the DOM**.

In *Chapter 2, Styling with CSS3*, we saw how to select parts of the DOM using CSS selectors. JavaScript has built-in functions to do so by using the traditional `document.getElementById` function. This function has a limited functionality and does not allow selecting from the DOM using the CSS selector syntax as the jQuery selectors do, however, now JavaScript includes `querySelector()` and `querySelectorAll()`. These two functions are more powerful and take CSS queries just as the jQuery selector syntax does. While the `querySelector()` function returns a single DOM element, the `querySelectorAll()` function returns a list of nodes. Both functions exist on the `document` and `element` objects. So, you can query the document to find all matching results in the entire document, or you can just query a single element to find all matching objects under it. For example:

```
var postDiv = document.querySelector('#postDiv);
var allDivs = postDiv.querySelectorAll('div');
```

Alongside these two JavaScript selection methods, the `WinJS.Utilities` namespace provides two functions with similar features for selecting elements, namely `id()` and `query()`. Basically, these functions wrap the `querySelector` and `querySelectorAll` functions but the return result value is different. The selector functions provided by `WinJS.Utilities` return a `QueryCollection` object, which in turn exposes various operations that perform actions over the elements of the collection, such as adding and removing a class and others.

The following code shows the syntax for using `id()` and `query()`. We first create a `WinJS.Utilities` object and call these two methods on it as shown:

```
var utils = WinJS.Utilities;
var postDiv = utils.id('postDiv');
var allParagraphs = utils.query('p');
allParagraphs.setStyle("color", "red");
```

The following screenshot shows the IntelliSense window that lists the functions provided by the `WinJS.Utilities` namespace:

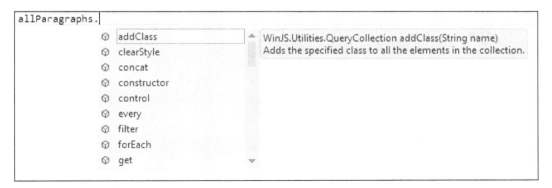

Querying the DOM is also useful when you need to apply a behavior to the elements of `document`. For example, you might want to add a functionality whenever the user clicks on a particular button. We do so by first querying for that element and then adding a `click` handler to it. The following code shows how:

```
WinJS.Utilities.id("Btn").listen("click", function () {
    var p = document.createElement("p");
    p.innerHTML = "i was just added";
    document.querySelector("#postDiv").appendChild(p);
});
```

In the previous code sample, the `listen()` method is used to wire an event handler to the `click` event of the button with the ID `Btn`; in this handler, we are creating a new p element and adding it to the `div` element with the ID `postDiv`.

 The methods provided by the `WinJS.Utilities` namespace are like a simplified subset of the functions provided in jQuery.

The following is a list of some of the available methods that you can call on the objects returned in `QueryCollection`:

- `addClass`
- `clearStyle`
- `getAttribute`
- `hasClass`
- `query(query)`
- `removeClass`
- `removeEventListener`
- `setAttribute`
- `setStyle`
- `toggleClass`
- `children`

Understanding WinJS.xhr

The xhr function basically wraps the calls to XMLHttpRequest in a Promise object. The function is useful for cross-domain and intranet requests, as shown in the following code:

```
WinJS.xhr(options).then(
    function completed(result) {
....
    },
    function error(result) {
....
    },
    function progress(result) {
....
    },
```

Since the WinJS.xhr function processes asynchronously and returns a Promise object, we can pass the then() or done() method to it, as shown in the previous example.

You can use the WinJs.xhr function to connect to a web service and to download different types of content, such as text or a JSON string that are specified in the responseType option of WinJS.xhr. The responseType option takes a string value that specifies the type of response expected from the request, and the types are as follows:

- text: This is the default value and expects a response of type string

- arraybuffer: This expects an **ArrayBuffer** used to represent binary content such as an array of type integer or float

- blob: This expects a **Blob** (**Binary Large Object**), which is an object that represents immutable raw data and is typically of a large file size

- document: This expects XML content; that is, content that has a MIME type of text/xml

- json: This expects a JSON string

- ms-stream: This expects an msStream object that handles streaming data and is marked with a vendor-specific prefix (ms) because it is not defined in the W3C specifications yet

Besides `responseType`, a couple of more options can be applied to the `xhr` (`XMLHttpRequest`) objects, which are all optional except `url`. These options are as follows:

- `url`: This specifies a string that is either the absolute or relative URL of the XML data or server-side XML web services

- `type`: This specifies a string that represents the HTTP method used; for example, GET, POST, or HEAD

- `user`: This specifies a string that represents the name of the user used for authentication, if required

- `password`: This specifies a string that represents the password used for authentication, if any

- `headers`: This specifies an object that represents a custom HTTP header

- `data`: This specifies an object that contains the data that will be sent with the HTTP request to the server; this data is passed directly to the `XMLHttpRequest.send` method

- `customRequestInitializer`: This specifies a function that can be used for preprocessing on `XMLHttpRequest`.

Let's populate the basic syntax on how to retrieve some text from a website as shown in the following code:

```
WinJS.xhr(
{ url: 'http://www.msdn.microsoft.com/library', responseType: 'text'
})
.done(function (request)
{
    var text = request.responseText;
    document.getElementById("responseDiv").innerHTML = text;
},
function error(request) {
  var errorStatus = "Error returned: " + request.statusText;
  document.getElementById("errorDiv").innerHTML = errorStatus;
});
```

The previous code sample will retrieve the text from the specified `url` string and insert it into the `div` element, `responseDiv`; in case there was an error during processing, we retrieve it in the error-handling function via `statusText`.

It is not recommended to use the `XMLHttpRequest` object to request a transfer of extremely large objects that might take a long time to complete, such as the **Blob** and the **FormData** objects. Instead, you should consider using the file upload APIs provided by the Windows Runtime API for such operations.

Introducing a new set of controls

Besides content, your app will need controls; regular HTML controls such as buttons, select lists, and checkboxes; and some Windows 8 exclusive controls such as the AppBar rating and settings. In addition to the standard built-in HTML controls, `WinJS` provides a set of new and feature-rich controls designed for Windows Store apps using JavaScript. These controls are basically objects available in the `WinJS.UI` namespace; so, a date picker control will look like `WinJS.UI.DatePicker`. Here is a list of the major `WinJS.UI` controls you will use in an app:

- `DatePicker`: This renders a customizable control that is used to select a date value

- `TimePicker`: This renders a customizable control that is used to select a time value

- `Menu`: This renders a menu flyout control for displaying commands

- `AppBar`: This renders an application toolbar for displaying commands

- `FlipView`: This renders a collection of items to be displayed one item at a time

- `ListView`: This renders a collection of items in a customizable grid or list layout

- `Flyout`: This is a control that displays a kind of a pop up control containing information; however, it is lightweight and doesn't create a separate window such as a dialog box

- `Rating`: This is a control that allows the user to rate something and can display three types of ratings—tentative, average, or the user's rating

- `SemanticZoom`: This is a control that lets the user zoom between a zoomed-in and zoomed-out view, which is supplied by two separate child controls that provide each type of view:

- `ToggleSwitch`: This renders a control that lets the user switch an option between two states (on and off)

- `Tooltip`: This renders a control that displays a tooltip to show more information about an object, and it can support rich content (such as images)

- `ViewBox`: This renders a control that scales a single child element it contains (without changing its aspect ratio) to make it fit and fill the available space

 These controls are automatically styled with either one of the two stylesheets that appear by default in any new Windows 8 Store app project you create in Visual Studio. The two stylesheets (one with a dark color theme and the other with a light one) will give your app the look and feel of Windows 8.

Unlike standard HTML controls, `WinJS.UI` controls do not have dedicated markup elements or attribute tags; for example, you can't go on adding a `WinJS.UI.Rating` element such as `<rating/>` to your markup, as you would normally do with the standard HTML elements such as `<input/>`. To add a `WinJS.UI` control, you need to create an HTML element, say `div`, and use the `data-win-control` attribute to specify the type of control you want. The following code shows the syntax to create a `WinJS.UI Rating` control:

```
<div id="ratingControlDiv" data-win-control="WinJS.UI.Rating"> </div>
```

This will declare a rating element in the markup but will not load the control in your app when you run it. In order to activate any `WinJS` control that you've declared in the markup, the JavaScript code must call the `WinJS.UI.processAll()` function that processes the document and initializes the controls you created. When you create an app using any of the templates provided in Visual Studio, the `default.js` file includes a call to `WinJS.UI.processAll` in the code, declared in the `app.onactivated` event handler.

When you run the app, you will see the new `Rating` control as follows:

You can also create a `WinJS` control in code by calling its constructor and passing the HTML element that will host this control to the constructor. For example, if we have `div` with an `id` attribute of `ratingControlDiv`, the JavaScript to create a `Rating` control will be as follows:

```
var ratingHost = document.getElementById("ratingControlDiv");
var ratingControl = new WinJS.UI.Rating(hostElement);
```

In this case, there will be no need to call the `WinJS.UI.processAll` function, since you didn't create the JavaScript control in the markup.

Also, setting the properties of a `WinJS` control differs from setting the properties of a standard HTML control; the latter has dedicated attributes for that purpose. For example, an `input` element of the type `range` has `min` and `max` attributes whose values can be set in the markup as shown in the following code:

```
<input type="range" min="2" max="10" />
```

In the case of a JavaScript control, we have to use the `data-win-options` attribute to set a property in the markup, which takes a string that contains one or more property/value pairs (multiple properties are separated with a comma) and in its basic form looks as shown in the following code:

```
data-win-options="{propertyName: propertyValue}"
```

The following syntax will show how to set the `minRating` and `maxRating` attributes for a `WinJS.UI.Rating` control:

```
<div id="ratingHostDiv" data-win-control="WinJS.UI.Rating"
    data-win-options="{ minRating: 2, maxRating: 10}">
</div>
```

Summary

We have glimpsed some of the capabilities and powerful features of the `WinJS` in Windows 8. We learned how to implement asynchronous programming using the `Promise` object.

Also, we were introduced to the methods provided in the `WinJS.Utilities` namespace that allow us to retrieve and modify the elements of an HTML document. We also covered retrieving different types of content with the `WinJS.xhr()` function.

Finally, we learned about the new set of controls provided by the WinJS library and how to create these JavaScript controls and set their properties.

In the next chapter, we will start developing apps with JavaScript by introducing the needed tools first and then learn about the templates provided for Windows 8 JavaScript apps. Also, we will create a very basic app and understand the anatomy of the JavaScript app. We will also learn about the ListView control.

4
Developing Apps with JavaScript

In this chapter we will learn how to get started with developing a Windows 8 app using JavaScript. First, we will learn about the tools and then we will cover how to acquire a developer license. Afterwards, we will start with one of the templates provided for Windows Store apps development, build a sample app from a blank template, and modify it so that we get to see to know some of the features of a JavaScript app.

Introducing the tools

Windows Store apps are a new type of application introduced by Windows 8 and run only on that platform. So, in order to start developing, you will first need to have Windows 8 installed on your machine and second, the required development tools.

There are two options for acquiring Windows 8; one option is to get it from the Subscriber Downloads on MSDN, if you have a subscription there. Alternatively, if you don't have an MSDN account, you can get the 90-day evaluation version of Windows 8 Enterprise from the *Evaluation Center*, found on the MSDN website via http://msdn.microsoft.com/en-US/evalcenter/jj554510.aspx?wt.mc_id=MEC_132_1_4.

 Note that the Evaluation Edition cannot be upgraded after expiry.

After installing Windows 8, you will need to download the developer tools, which are available for free on the *Windows Dev Center* page on the MSDN site. The Windows Dev Center, with its new and improved layout, is your starting point for all the tools and resources you might need and can be found under the section **Downloads for developing Windows Store apps** at `http://msdn.microsoft.com/en-US/windows/apps/br229516.aspx`.

The essential download is the bundle containing Visual Studio Express, which will be your tool to develop Windows apps. The link to this download is available under the **Visual Studio Express 2012 for Windows 8** section and contains the following files:

- Microsoft Visual Studio Express 2012 for Windows 8
- Blend for Microsoft Visual Studio 2012
- Windows 8 software development kit (SDK)
- Windows Store apps project templates (available within Visual Studio 2012)

Additionally, you can find other available downloads on that page, such as:

- Design assets: This includes the necessary Photoshop templates (`.psd` files), which include templates, common controls, and common components such as contracts, notifications, and tiles needed for designing an app.
- Sample App Pack: This includes hundreds of code samples from Microsoft to help jump-start your project quickly and learn about most of the features. This is available in all or specific programming languages.
- Hands-on labs for Windows 8: This includes a series of eight hands-on lab modules, which in turn guide you through the development of a Windows Store app titled Contoso Cookbook. This incorporates many of the key new features available in Windows 8. These lab series are available in JavaScript and HTML, or C# and **Extensible Application Markup Language** (**XAML**).
- Live SDK: This includes a set of controls and APIs that we can use to enable the app to integrate **Single Sign-on** (**SSO**) with a Microsoft account and access information from SkyDrive, Hotmail, and Windows Live Messenger.

Since Windows Store app development in Visual Studio 2012 is only supported on Windows 8, you cannot develop apps on Windows 7 even if you have Visual Studio 2012 installed. Moreover, you can't develop Windows Store apps on Windows Server 2012 since the developer licenses aren't available for it.

Note that you can use any of the other Visual Studio 2012 editions to develop Windows Store apps, including the Ultimate, Premium, Professional, and Test Professional editions.

Getting a free developer license

In order to start developing Windows Store apps, you will need to have a developer license for Windows 8. This license lets you install, develop, test, and evaluate apps locally before they are tested and certified by the Windows Store. Moreover, the developer licenses are free and you do not need a Store account to get one; it only requires a Microsoft account and you can acquire more than one license per account. It expires in 30 days and must be renewed. If you already have a Windows Store account, the license will serve you for 90 days. After you acquire a license on a local machine, you won't be prompted again on that machine unless it expires, or you remove it (maybe by formatting or uninstalling Visual Studio). It is quite easy to get one; you can get a developer license using Visual Studio 2012. When you run it for the first time on Windows 8, it will prompt you to obtain a developer license; all you need to do is to sign in with your Microsoft account. You can always attempt to acquire or renew a developer license for Windows 8 from inside Visual Studio using the store options, which we will discuss in more details in *Chapter 10, Packaging and Publishing*, when we learn about publishing the app.

Bear in mind that the first time you try to run an app, you will be prompted to acquire a developer license if you haven't already done so.

The following screenshot shows the process using Visual Studio 2012 Ultimate.
Go to **Project | Store | Acquire Developer License**.

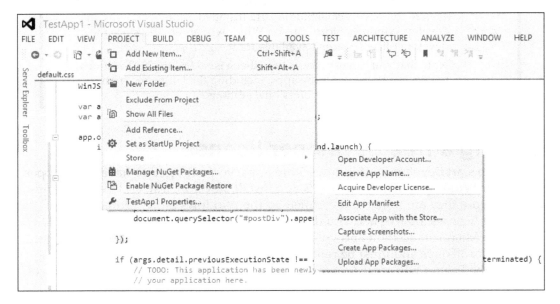

If you're using the Express edition, you will have a **Store** option directly in the top menu, not underneath **Project**. You simply have to go to **Store | Acquire Developer License**.

 Choosing not to acquire or renew a developer license will result in an error (code DEP0100) when you try to build or deploy the app in Visual Studio.

After you install Windows 8 and the required tools and obtain a developer license, you're ready to start building your first app. You start by choosing a programming language to use. As we previously mentioned, Windows 8 allows you to build on your programming language knowledge base and develop with the languages you already know (unless you want to learn something new). If you are into web development, you can choose JavaScript as your programming language and use the latest technologies in web development (HTML5 and CSS3, to name a few), and that's what this book is all about. If you're coming from a .NET background, you can choose Visual C# or Visual Basic and XAML. And you have the C++ option with either C++ and XAML or C++ and DirectX.

Using Visual Studio and its templates

So we now have the tools. With Visual Studio as our playground and JavaScript as our programming language, we are set and ready to develop. We will start by creating a new project for Windows Store. Go to **File | New Project**. Drill down under **Installed**, go to **Templates** and then to **JavaScript | Windows Store**, and select a template type as the following screenshot shows:

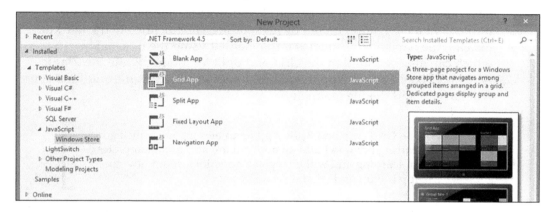

As you see in the previous screenshot, on the center pane of the **New Project** dialog there are five templates to choose from. These templates come with Visual Studio 2012 and provide a good starting point and help you jump-start and speed up the development of your apps. These project templates, as per their order of appearance on the **New Project** dialog, are as follows:

- **Blank App**: This is a basic project template that creates an empty Windows Store app that compiles and runs. However, it contains no user interface controls or data.

- **Grid App**: This is a project that provides a grid view format of the content. It is a good starting point for an app that allows users to browse through categories of data to find content. A few examples of its use include RSS readers, shopping apps, news apps, and media gallery apps.

- **Split App**: This is a project that provides a split view of the content, whereby the data is displayed in a two-column master/detail view with the list of data on one side and the details of each single data item on the other side, just as in Outlook. A few examples of its uses include news reader apps, sports scores apps, and e-mail apps.

- **Fixed Layout App**: This is a project with a basic and minimal template, similar to an app created with the **Blank App** template, but the difference is that the content in this layout is aimed at the fixed-layout viewport, whereby the container is automatically resized when the window size changes to conform to the display area; this scaling is ensured using the `ViewBox` control.

- **Navigation App**: This is a project that creates an app with the single-page navigation model recommended for Windows Store apps. You cannot implement a navigation model by just adding `anchor` links to the markup; instead, the navigation model is implemented using the `navigator.js` file, which can also be found in the Grid and Split templates, while the **Blank App** and **Fixed Layout App** templates do not include this file and thus you will have to add the file manually.

> The **Grid App** and **Split App** templates are not only a good starting point to build an app, but are also great templates for learning and will give you a good idea about how the app is built and what it is composed of.

The three templates **Blank App**, **Grid App**, and **Split App** are shared between all the available programming languages for Windows Store development. Each project template includes the necessary files needed to implement the feature it represents without any development from your side; for example, creating a new Grid App and running it will result in the following app:

The result is a Windows Store-ready app that contains dummy data with navigation enabled and even supports **snapped and fill layouts**, which are the layouts that apps exist in when the resolution is split between two apps that are side by side. All of this without even writing a single line of code! So, imagine if you customize this minimal app a little by applying different styles to the layout and display real data in the content (say, RSS feeds from a news website), you will have a news app that is more than 75 percent ready for the Store (missing a couple of features such as semantic zoom, app bar, and settings) in no time.

You can also download samples directly from Visual Studio. These samples will provide completed and working code samples that will compile and run as a Windows Store app, with the purpose of demonstrating the various new programming models, platforms, features, and components available in Windows 8.

Project item templates

In addition to the project templates, you have language-specific item templates exclusive to Windows Store apps, in our case, called **JavaScript item templates**. These item templates are app files that can be added to an already existing project and contain commonly used code and functionality (consider it a user control), and also help to reduce development time. Item templates can be added by right-clicking on **Project** from the top menu and then going to **Add | New Item**. There are four JavaScript item templates available; they are as follows:

- **Page Control**: This contains the basic content and markup for a page in the app, which includes a header section with a Back button and a main content section. Each **Page Control** template will include three files to be added to the project (an HTML file containing the markup needed, a JavaScript file containing the code related for the page, and a CSS file that provides the style specific to the page).

- **File Open Picker Contract**: This will add the functionality that enables an app to provide its data as a file list to other requesting apps using a **File Picker** dialog. It will also display the files in a ListView control. A typical use for this would be when creating a photo-picker dialog.

- **Search Contract**: This will add the search contract that allows the app to respond to search queries coming from Search Charm in Windows 8. It contains a search results page to present the results to the user. It is important to add this contract if your app has some data that can be searched for.

- **Share Target Contract**: This will add the share contract to the app, which enables an app to expose data for sharing with other apps and make it integrate with Share Charm in Windows 8. So, if the app has this contract, it will appear in the list of apps in the Share UI. A typical use for this template would be to allow users to post links or photos to Facebook, Twitter, or any other app that receives shared content. Vice versa, it will also enable the app to receive shared content; thus, the app can behave like Facebook or Twitter.

The following screenshot shows the **Add New Item** dialog with the previously listed project item templates:

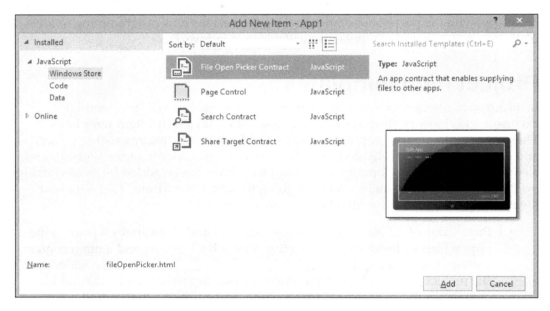

I recommend you add each item template to a separate folder with a correlated name. Since each item template adds three related files, the solution will be neater and more organized if you group them into separate folders. For example, a folder for pages and under it a folder for each page; the same goes for the contracts.

After you chose an app template and it was loaded onto Visual Studio, you would have basically created a very simple app; this app can directly compile and run. Using Visual Studio, you can run the app either on your local machine or on the Simulator. To run it on your local machine, simply press *F5* to build, deploy, and start the app.

Note that you can instead just deploy the solution but the app will not run directly; you will need to find it among the other apps in the Start menu and launch it manually instead.

There is a third option to run a remote device connected directly through an Ethernet cable. To use the simulator, you only need to select from the options in the run menu as shown in the following screenshot:

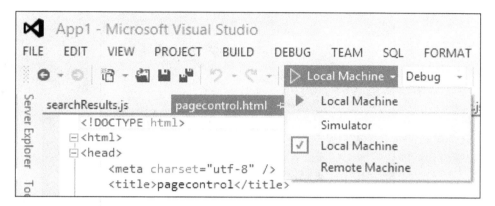

The Windows 8 Simulator is a great tool to help you test and debug the app; it allows you to test the features as if you were working with the real device, especially if you do not have a tablet or a touch-enabled device during development. It will enable the app to change resolutions and screen orientations between landscape and portrait and toggle between the different app layouts and view states (snapped and full). In addition, you can test how the app responds to touch and gestures such as swipe and pinch to zoom. We wouldn't be able to try all these features and functionalities on a laptop or PC during development.

 When you run the app in Visual Studio in the debug mode, you can make changes to the code and markup and refresh the app to see the changes without having to rebuild/rerun it. You can do this using the **Refresh Windows App** button, which will appear next to the pause, stop, and restart debugging buttons, only after you run the app from within Visual Studio.

Getting started with Blank App

Let's start creating a minimal app using the **Blank App** template; the first thing we need to do is launch Visual Studio 2012, create a new project, and go to **JavaScript | Windows Store | Blank App**. Although the Blank App seems empty when you run it, it contains several files that are essential to any Windows Store app you create using JavaScript; all the other templates will have these files. The following screenshot shows the structure of this app listed in the **Solution Explorer** window:

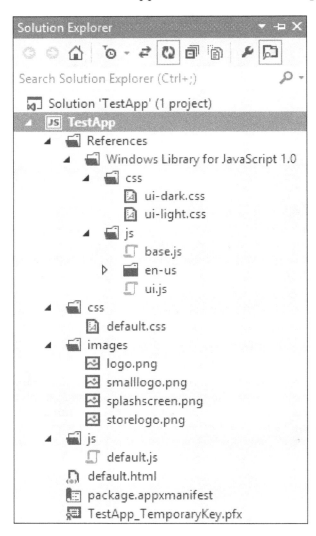

This previous screenshot shows the skeleton of a simple app, with the following files:

- `Windows Library for JavaScript 1.0`: The Windows Library for JavaScript is a library of CSS and JavaScript files. As you drill down into this folder you will see that it contains two subfolders, as follows:
  - `css`: This folder includes the two main CSS stylesheets that contains the set of styles that gives the app the Windows 8 look and feel. The two stylesheets are `ui-dark.css` and `ui-light.css`. As their names imply, the first will apply a dark color theme to the app and the latter a light color. You can choose either one by referencing it in the HTML pages.
  - `js`: This folder includes `base.js` and `ui.js`; these two files contain the JavaScript APIs that provide the controls, objects, and helper functions, all organized into namespaces that will make the development experience using JavaScript much easier.
- `default.css`: This is the stylesheet that contains the CSS styles for the app.
- `images`: This folder contains the images needed to present the app and its identity (two logos, the splash screen image, and the store logo).
- `default.js`: This JavaScript file implements the main functionality of the app and contains the code that handles your app's life cycle. In this file, you can write any additional code that is related to the `default.html` page.
- `default.html`: This is the start and home page that is first loaded when the app runs. It provides the markup for the content host (where each page is loaded into the main window).
- `package.appxmanifest`: This is the manifest file. It basically describes the app package for Windows by specifying the properties that describe an app, such as name, description, start page, and so on.
- `TestApp_TemporaryKey.pfx` (`AppName_TemporaryKey.pfx`): This file signs the `.appxmanifest` file.

Let's have a look at the `default.html` page, which is the start page of the app (and in this case, the only page):

```
<!DOCTYPE html>
<html>
<head>
  <meta charset="utf-8" />
  <title>TestApp</title>
```

```
    <!-- WinJS references -->
    <link href="//Microsoft.WinJS.1.0/css/ui-dark.css" rel="stylesheet"
/>
    <script src="//Microsoft.WinJS.1.0/js/base.js"></script>
    <script src="//Microsoft.WinJS.1.0/js/ui.js"></script>

    <!-- TestApp references -->
    <link href="/css/default.css" rel="stylesheet" />
    <script src="/js/default.js"></script>
  </head>
  <body>
    <p>Content goes here</p>
  </body>
</html>
```

As you can tell from `Doctype html`, the page is HTML5. We have the title of the
app in the `<head>` and then the reference for the Windows Library for JavaScript
(`WinJS`) files. The references are marked with the comment `WinJS references`.
The `.css` file is referenced first so that the loading of the scripts doesn't delay or
hinder the loading of the styles and, in case the `.js` files apply some modifications
to the stylesheet, the styles need to be loaded beforehand. The dark color theme
is applied; you can simply change it to the light one by changing the reference
as follows:

```
<link href="//Microsoft.WinJS.1.0/css/ui-light.css" rel="stylesheet" />
```

> Try not to modify the CSS and JavaScript files of `WinJS`.
> It is better to create styles or JavaScript functions that
> override existing styles and functionalities in different
> files and apply them to the app.

Under the `WinJS` references, there are references to the stylesheets and JavaScript
files that are app-specific and clearly differentiated by the comment.

Then comes the body. Here, in the example of a blank app, the body contains
nothing but simple text.

If you attempt to launch the app as is, you will see a black color background covering
the screen and will also see the text: **Content goes here**. And just before this page
appears, you will notice that a splash screen appears for a few seconds, displaying
the image specified for the splash screen in the manifest file. Let's try to put some
life into this blank app by modifying our start page and adding some markup to
the body, just as you would add to any HTML page you've dealt with before.

Replace the existing paragraph element with the following:

```
<body>
  <h1>The Test App</h1>
  <p>Add some content </p>
  <input id="contentInput" type="text" />
  <button id="sayButton">Have your say</button>
  <div id="contentOutput"></div>
</body>
```

Run the app; it will display the markup we just added. We can type in any text in the `input` element but clicking the button will have no effect. So let's create an event handler for this button to output in `div` whatever we add in the `input` element. We need to create the event handler in the `default.js` file because it's where we write the additional code that interacts with the `default.html` page.

First let's have a look at this `default.js` file. You will notice some code inside it wrapped by a single function, shown as follows:

```
(function () {
  "use strict";
  ...
})();
```

This code represents a self-executing anonymous function that wraps all your code to avoid any naming conflicts and keeps the global namespace clean of unnecessary identifiers. The first line of code in the anonymous function declares the keyword `use strict`, which turns on the strict mode for the JavaScript code. This strict mode provides better error-checking, such as preventing you from assigning a value to a read-only property. After this line, you will see the rest of the code, which handles the activated and checkpoint states of the app by adding the `app.onactivated` and `app.oncheckpoint` event handlers. The code we add inside the `app.onactivated` event handler will be added when the app starts.

Now back to the button event handler; let's create a function as follows:

```
function buttonClickHandler(eventInfo) {
  var text = document.getElementById("contentInput").value;
  var outputString = "I say " + text + "!";
  document.getElementById("contentOutput").innerText = outputString;
}
```

Add this function inside the anonymous function before the app.start() call at the bottom line. This function retrieves the text from the input element and adds it to the div element. To add this function to the events of the button (in this case, the onclick event), we need to register an event handler with the button. The recommended way to do so is by calling the addEventListener method. We need to register this event handler when the app gets activated. So, we should add it inside the app.onactivated event handler. And the code will look as follows:

```
var app = WinJS.Application;
var activation = Windows.ApplicationModel.Activation;

app.onactivated = function (args) {
  if (args.detail.kind === activation.ActivationKind.launch) {
      if (args.detail.previousExecutionState !== activation.
ApplicationExecutionState.terminated) {
        // TODO: This application has been newly launched. Initialize
          // your application here.
    } else {
    // TODO: This application has been reactivated from suspension.
    // Restore application state here.
      }
      args.setPromise(WinJS.UI.processAll());

      // Retrieve the button and register our event handler.
      var sayButton = document.getElementById("sayButton");
      sayButton.addEventListener("click", buttonClickHandler, false);
  }
};
```

The app variable is a global variable representing an instance of the Application class that provides application-level functionality; for example, handling different application events such as the onactivated event that we saw in the previous code listing.

Inside the onactivated handler, the code checks to see the type of activation that has occurred; in this case, it is a launch activation, which means that this app was activated by the user when it was not running. Then a call is made to WinJS.UI.processAll().This will scan the default.html file for any WinJS controls and will initialize them. Since the button is not a WinJS control and rather a basic HTML control, we could add it before the call to WinJS.UI.processAll(), but it's good practice to register the event handlers after it.

Run the app, enter some text in the textbox, and the content is displayed when the button is clicked, as the following screenshot shows:

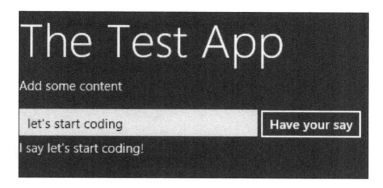

Understanding the ListView control

In the previous chapter we introduced a new set of controls provided by the Windows Library for JavaScript; one of these controls was the ListView control, marked as `WinJS.UI.ListView`. What this object basically does is displays data items in a customizable list or grid. To create a ListView control, we need to add the `data-win-control` property to a `div` element and set its property to `WinJS.UI.ListView`. In the `default.html` page, add the following code inside the body tag:

```
<body>
  <div id="sampleListView" data-win-control="WinJS.UI.ListView">
  </div>
</body>
```

This will create an empty ListView. So, if we run the app, there will be nothing to see. Since it is a `WinJS` control, it will not be rendered in the markup until after we call the `WinJS.UI.processAll` function.

Let's add some data for the `sampleListView` control to display. The data that might come from a database from the Web or from a JSON data source, will create a data source manually, and preferably in a separate JavaScript file so it would be easier to maintain. So, in Visual Studio, under the `js` folder, add a new item and select a JavaScript file; name it `data.js`. Open this newly created file and create an anonymous function with the strict mode on, just as we saw in the `default.js` file; inside this function, let's create a sample array of objects that make up the data source we need. Give each object in the array the three properties `firstName`, `lastName`, and `Age`.

The resulting code will look as follows:

```
(function () {
    "use strict";
    //create an array for a sample data source
    var dataArray = [
    { name: "John Doe", country: "England", age: "28" },
    { name: "Jane Doe", country: "England", age: "20" },
    { name: "Mark Wallace", country: "USA", age: "34" },
    { name: "Rami Rain", country: "Lebanon", age: "18" },
    { name: "Jean Trops", country: "France", age: "56" }

    ];

    //create a list object from the array
    var sampleDataList = new WinJS.Binding.List(dataArray);
})();
```

Next, we use the array we just created to create a List object; then we need to expose this List object by declaring a namespace for it and adding the List as a public member:

```
// Create a namespace to make the data publicly
// accessible.
var publicMembers =
    {
        itemList: sampleDataList
    };
WinJS.Namespace.define("DataSample", publicMembers);
```

In order for the ListView control to be able to access this List, we used the `WinJS.Namespace.define` function to create a namespace and add the List as one of its members, thus making the List publicly accessible since it is created in an anonymous function, which keeps it private. The `WinJS.Namespace.define` function takes two parameters, as you noticed in the previous code. The first parameter is the name of the namespace to create, and the second represents the object (`publicMembers`) that contains one or more key/value pairs.

After creating the data source and making it accessible by the ListView control, the next thing is to connect the data source to the ListView control. That has to be done in the `default.html` file. Let's pick up from where we left our sample blank app. We need to add a reference to the data file we just created, as follows:

```
<!-- Sample data file. -->
<script src="/js/data.js"></script>
```

We then add the `data-win-options` attribute to the `div` element and use the data source we created inside `data.js` to set the `itemDataSource` property inside the `data-win-options` attribute. Set the ListView control's `itemDataSource` property to `DataSample.itemList.dataSource` as follows:

```
<div id="sampleListView" data-win-control="WinJS.UI.ListView"
 data-win-options="{ itemDataSource : DataSample.itemList.dataSource
}">
</div>
```

The `DataSample.itemList.dataSource` namespace comprises `DataSample`, which is the namespace we registered previously; `itemList`, which is the name of the property defined on the object we registered on the namespace; and finally `dataSource`, which is a property of the `WinJS.Binding.List` method (we are able to call it on `itemList` because the latter was assigned to the List object we created from the array).

If we run the app now, we will see that the ListView control displays the array we created with no formatting, as follows:

```
{ name: "John Doe", country: "England", age: "28" }
{ name: "Jane Doe", country: "England", age: "20" }
{ name: "Mark Wallace", country: "USA", age: "34" }
{ name: "Rami Rain", country: "Lebanon", age: "18" }
{ name: "Jean Trops", country: "France", age: "56" }
```

We can style this ListView control by overriding the default styles set in the `win-listview` class, which is defined by the Windows Library for JavaScript, to style the ListView control. In order to override the default styles and apply some to just this ListView control, copy the `win-listview` class and precede it with the specific ID of the `div` element we created, as follows:

```
#sampleListView.win-listview {
  width: 500px;
  border: 1px solid gray;
}
```

We can add more styling to the ListView elements inside and we can define an item template using `WinJS.Binding.Template`, which is used to define the markup we want to use to display each list item and its styles. It is very easy to create a `WinJS.Binding.Template` control; in the HTML page, add a `div` element and set the property of the data attribute `data-win-control` to `WinJS.Binding.Template`. Inside it, add another `div` element that will serve as a parent for the template's contents, because `WinJS.Binding.Template` must have a single root element. Inside this parent element, we add the markup that we will create, which the ListView will use to populate each data item it contains. Now the template will look like this:

```html
<body>
<div id="sampleTemplate" data-win-control="WinJS.Binding.Template">
    <div style="width:200px; height: 100px">
        <div>
            <!-- Displays the "name" field. -->
            <h2> </h2>
            <!-- Displays the "country" field. -->
            <h3> </h3>
            <!-- Displays the "age" field. -->
            <h6 style="color:red"> </h6>
        </div>
    </div>
</div>
</body>
```

In order to link each element to a specific data item property, we use the `data-win-bind` attribute on each element that displays data. The `data-win-bind` attribute uses this syntax: `data-win-bind="propertyName: dataFieldName"`. Hence, to set the name property on the `h2`, `h3`, and `h6` elements, we use the following code:

```html
<!-- Displays the "name" field. -->
<h2 data-win-bind="innerText: name"></h2>
<!-- Displays the "age" field. -->
<h3 data-win-bind="innerText: country"></h3>
<!-- Displays the "age" field. -->
<h6 style="color:red" data-win-bind="innerText: age"></h6>
```

It is important to note that the list item template (`WinJS.Binding.Template`) should be before the ListView control in the markup, simply because the HTML markup is hierarchical and each UI element will be rendered as it is being encountered. So, when the ListView control is being rendered and is bound to an `itemTemplate` element, that `itemTemplate` element must exist first; otherwise it will throw an error.

Finally, we need to apply the binding template we just created on the ListView control. Thus, use the `select` syntax to set the `itemTemplate` property of the ListView to sampleTemplate, as follows:

```
<div id="sampleListView" data-win-control="WinJS.UI.ListView"
data-win-options="{ itemDataSource : DataSample.itemList.dataSource,
itemTemplate: select('#sampleTemplate') }">
</div>
```

If we run the app now, the ListView control will display the data in a more presentable manner. Here is how it will look:

Summary

Throughout this chapter we have covered the basics for creating a Windows Store app using JavaScript. We got introduced to the tools, and what we need to get going with the development. Then we went over using Visual Studio 2012 and we got to have a look at the templates provided for the development using JavaScript.

We saw how to build an app from scratch and on the way we got to see the anatomy of a JavaScript Windows Store app; we modified this blank app to make it interact in the simplest way possible, at the click of a button. Finally, we learned how to use the ListView control to display data.

In the next chapter we will learn how to get the data that we want to display.

5
Binding Data to the App

In this chapter we will learn how to implement data binding from different data sources to the elements in the app. The Windows library for JavaScript provides the data source objects that can be used to populate the WinJS controls such as ListView or FlipView with different sorts of data. We have the WinJS.Binding.List object that is used to access arrays and JSON data and the StorageDataSource object that provides access to information about the filesystem. These two data source objects enable us to query and bind to items in the data source. Additionally, we will learn how to apply sorting and filtering on the data source and display its data using the ListView control.

Getting the data

The **Windows library for JavaScript binding** (WinJS.Binding) provides a mechanism to bind data and styles to the HTML elements. The binding provided by the Windows library for JavaScript is one-way by default, so the HTML elements are updated when the data changes; however, any change in the HTML elements does not reflect on the data being bound to. Let's see this in action, and we'll start with the very basic kind of binding; that is, a declarative binding between an HTML element and a simple JavaScript object that contains only data.

First we will check for the WinJS.Binding.optimizeBindingReferences property, and set it to true if not set already.

 It is important to always set the WinJS.Binding. optimizeBindingReferences property to true while performing a declarative binding. This property determines whether or not the binding should automatically set the ID of an element. This property should be set to true in apps that use WinJS.Binding.

We'll create a sample `person` JavaScript object that contains two properties, `name` and `badgeColor`, as shown in the following code:

```
var person = { name: "John", badgeColor: "Blue"};
```

Now we'll bind an HTML `span` element to the `person` object using the data attribute `data-win-bind`, as shown in the following code:

```
<span id="nameSpan" data-win-bind="innerText: name"></span>
```

In order for the binding to take place and consequently have the name appear in the `span` element, we must call the `WinJS.Binding.processAll()` method and pass it the DOM element and the `dataContext` object; it will start searching for the `data-win-bind` attribute at this specified element and then go through all the descendants of that element.

The following code retrieves the `span` element from the DOM and then passes the parameters to the `WinJS.Binding.processAll()` method:

```
var nameSpan = document.getElementById("nameSpan");
WinJS.Binding.processAll(nameSpan, person);
```

 If you are using the default.HTML page for this example, you will need to add the code after the call to `args.setPromise(WinJS.UI.processAll())` has been made so that all the controls have been initialized, as explained in *Chapter 3, JavaScript for Windows Apps*.

Run the project and you will see the name **John** on the screen. The preceding code implements only a static binding, which means the text is not affected by the change in data. This is because a JavaScript object by itself is not capable of notifying the application when it changes. We can use `WinJS.Binding.as` to change this object to an observable object, which will enable the data source to get notified when items in that object change. The following code snippet will create a `bindingSource` object that manifests an observable instance of the `person` object we created; hence, any change made to `bindingSource` will be reflected in the HTML element it is bound to:

```
var bindingSource = WinJS.Binding.as(person);
```

Let's see this dynamic data binding in action. First, add an `input type` element to enter name values and a `button` element, as shown in the following code as shown in the following code:

```
<input type="text" id="nameInpt" />
<button id="setNameBtn">Get name</button>
```

Then, we write the code that simulates a change in the `person` data object. We do this by setting the `name` property in the `person` object to the new value entered in the `input` element on the click event for the `setNameBtn` button, as shown in the following code:

```
document.getElementById("setNameBtn").onclick = function () {
  var newName = document.getElementById("nameInpt").value;
  bindingSource.name = newName;
}
```

Run the project and try entering new values in the `input` element, and then click on the button to see the names getting changed.

Not only can we bind data to an HTML element but we can also apply binding at the level of the style. Going back to the previous example, let's add the `style.background` value to the data attribute and bind it to the `badgeColor` field of the `person` object, as shown in the following code:

```
data-win-bind="innerHTML: name; style.background: badgeColor"
```

Make the preceding changes and refresh the app, and the name will be highlighted in blue. When you run the app, the output should look like the following screenshot (if you are referencing the `ui-light.css` style sheet, the output will be a darker shade of blue):

There are several other approaches for data access and storage in Windows Store apps; the data sources can be either local or remote and your choice of storage basically depends on the scenario at hand. For example, a Windows Store app that needs to be connected and alive would require access to data from a remote online source. The data might be fetched from the web URLs or RESTful services. The ideal way to consume these web services is using the `WinJS.xhr` function that we were introduced to in *Chapter 3, JavaScript for Windows Apps*.

The WinJS.xhr function will make an asynchronous request to a web URL or a service and return the data in response upon a successful call. Let's assume we need to get some tweets and parse the results; the call is pretty straightforward in this case. To do this, provide the URL to the Twitter search service that will search for all the tweets that contain windows 8, as shown in the following code:

```
WinJS.xhr({
url: "http://search.twitter.com/search.json?q=windows8"}).then(
function (result) {
});
```

The output will be all the tweets that match the query wrapped in a JSON string, which is the data format provided by many websites. Windows 8 JavaScript has native support for JSON; hence, we can simply deserialize the JSON string into an object by calling JSON.parse(jsonString). Let's append the preceding code to get the following code:

```
WinJS.xhr({
  url: "http://search.twitter.com/search.json?q=windows8"}).then(
  function (result) {
    var jsonData = JSON.parse(result.responseText);
  });
```

We can also read the data from a file by using the Windows.Storage API file provided by Windows. If we have a readable file and an instance of storageFile that represents it, we can read the text from the file or we can read bytes using a buffer. In order to read text from a file, we can make use of the readTextAsync(file) function of the fileIO class as shown in the following code:

```
Windows.Storage.FileIO.readTextAsync(sampleFile).then(
function (fileContents) {
// some code to process the text read from the file
});
```

When the preceding code runs successfully, this function returns the contents of the file as a text string passed via the variable fileContents.

Almost the same thing applies when reading a byte from a file; however, we call the method readTextAsync(file) and pass it the file. We can then capture the buffer data in the response after the async process completes using the then() or done() method, as shown in the following code:

```
Windows.Storage.FileIO.readBufferAsync(sampleFile).then(
function (buffer) {
```

```
var bufferData = Windows.Storage.Streams.DataReader.
fromBuffer(buffer);
});
```

In the preceding code, we used the `DataReader` class to read from the buffer; this class provides the functionality to read strings from an in-memory stream and process the buffer.

Displaying the data

We have learned about the different sources of data and seen a couple of examples on how to get the data. Now we will see how to format and display that data. In the previous examples, we saw how we can bind data to any HTML element, but fortunately there is a better way to do this. The better way is using the Windows library for JavaScript, which provides controls and templates that make it easy to format and display the data. The most famous controls are `ListView` and `FlipView`; when it comes to binding and displaying data, the same technique applies for both but we'll use `ListView` in this chapter. It is not out of personal preference but a question of taking advantage of the features of `ListView` control, since it provides a flexible way to display data with built-in support for the cross-slide (touch) gesture; also, it is performance-optimized. Moreover, it delivers an appearance and a behavior that are consistent with Windows Store apps. The steps to do the binding and displaying the data are as follows:

1. Get the data.
2. Create a `WinJS.Binding.List` object to wrap the data.
3. Create a `ListView` element.
4. Set `itemDataSource` of the `ListView` element to the `WinJS.Binding.List` object.

Let's continue with the example we used previously for getting tweets via the web URL; the code returns a JSON string that is our data here, so the next step is to create a `WinJS.Binding.List` object as follows:

```
WinJS.xhr({
    url: "http://search.twitter.com/search.json?q=windows8"}).then(
    function (result) {
        var jsonData = JSON.parse(result.responseText);
        //create a binding list object from the json
        var bindingList = new WinJS.Binding.List(json.results);
    });
```

We just did steps 1 and 2; step 3 involves creating a `ListView` element in the DOM and getting an instance of it in the JavaScript code.

In HTML, we use the following:

```
<div id="sampleListView" data-win-control="WinJS.UI.ListView" >
</div>
```

In JavaScript, we use the following:

```
//get an instance of the ListView Control
var listView = document.getElementById("sampleListView").winControl;
```

In step 4, we set the `itemDataSource` attribute of the `ListView` object to `dataSource` of the `bindingList` object and the complete code will look like the following code snippet:

```
WinJS.xhr({
    url: "http://search.twitter.com/search.json?q=windows8"}).then(
    function (result) {
      var jsonData = JSON.parse(result.responseText);
      //create a binding list object from the json
      var bindingList = new WinJS.Binding.List(jsonData.results);
      //get the list view element from the DOM
      var listView =
      document.getElementById("sampleListView").winControl;
      //bind the data sources
      listView.itemDataSource = bindingList.dataSource
    });
```

If you are adding the `ListView` control or any other `WinJS.UI` control in the `default.html` page, remember to add the previous code in a `then()` or `done()` call on the function `WinJS.UI.ProcessAll()`, as shown in the following code:

```
args.setPromise(WinJS.UI.processAll().then(function () {
    //get the list view element from the DOM
    var listView =
    document.getElementById("sampleListView").winControl;
    //bind the data sources
    listView.itemDataSource = bindingList.dataSource
}));
```

The reason for adding that code is that this function processes the Windows library for JavaScript controls and renders these controls in the DOM.

Now let's build and run the project. The output will be a list containing the tweets, each with its properties, as shown in the following screenshot:

["created_at":"Tue, 07 May 2013 20:40:48 +0000","from_user":"hatiwin","from_user_id":900893773,"from_user_id_str":"900893773","fron
["result_type":"recent"),"profile_image_url":"http://a0.twimg.com/profile_images/2756679976/056c8e865fde10ac34f18619f5914531_norn
href="http://dlvr.it">dlvr.it</a>","text":"amazon:Windows8 上級マニュアル 上巻 http://t.co/owXITI0OWP #windows8

["created_at":"Tue, 07 May 2013 20:40:48 +0000","from_user":"hatiwin","from_user_id":900893773,"from_user_id_str":"900893773","fron
["result_type":"recent"),"profile_image_url":"http://a0.twimg.com/profile_images/2756679976/056c8e865fde10ac34f18619f5914531_norn
href="http://dlvr.it">dlvr.it</a>","text":"Yahoo!オークション:Windows8 Enterprise Pro 64bit 32bit 他多数最安値 !1 現在

["created_at":"Tue, 07 May 2013 20:40:47 +0000","from_user":"hatiwin","from_user_id":900893773,"from_user_id_str":"900893773","fron
["result_type":"recent"),"profile_image_url":"http://a0.twimg.com/profile_images/2756679976/056c8e865fde10ac34f18619f5914531_norn
href="http://dlvr.it">dlvr.it</a>","text":"楽天市場:SONY SVF15218CJW(ホワイト) VAIO Fit 15E http://t.co/AuMxpd2512

["created_at":"Tue, 07 May 2013 20:40:47 +0000","from_user":"hatiwin","from_user_id":900893773,"from_user_id_str":"900893773","fron
["result_type":"recent"),"profile_image_url":"http://a0.twimg.com/profile_images/2756679976/056c8e865fde10ac34f18619f5914531_norn
href="http://dlvr.it">dlvr.it</a>","text":"楽天市場:SONY SVD11239CJB VAIO Duo 11 http://t.co/h0McqL41u1 #windo

["created_at":"Tue, 07 May 2013 20:40:47 +0000","from_user":"hatiwin","from_user_id":900893773,"from_user_id_str":"900893773","fron
["result_type":"recent"),"profile_image_url":"http://a0.twimg.com/profile_images/2756679976/056c8e865fde10ac34f18619f5914531_norn
href="http://dlvr.it">dlvr.it</a>","text":"楽天市場:SONY SVF15217CJW(ホワイト) VAIO Fit 15E http://t.co/AMQ50YIHT

Although the `ListView` control does the job of binding the data automatically, it looks messed up and needs formatting. The `WinJS` control provides templates that can be used in combination with the `ListView` and `FlipView` objects to specify how each item should be displayed and which data it will show. Templates can be defined declaratively as a `WinJS` control and provide its structure and styles, either by specifying the `div` element in which it should appear or by using the `render` method to create its own `div` element. Let's see this in action. Inside the DOM, add a `div` element and assign it to `WinJS.Binding.Template` via the `data-win-control` attribute as follows:

```
<div id="listTemplate" data-win-control="WinJS.Binding.Template"></
div>
```

Then create the internal structure of the template by first adding a root `div` element and then adding the bound elements inside that root `div`, as shown in the following code snippet:

```
<div id="listTemplate" data-win-control="WinJS.Binding.Template">
  <div class="templateItem" style ="width:300px; height:100px;">
    <img src="#" style="float:left; width: 60px; height: 60px;"
      data-win-bind="src: profile_img_url" />
    <b>From:</b><span data-win-bind="innerText:
            from_user_name"></span>
```

```
      <br />
      <b>Date:</b><span data-win-bind="innerText:
              created_at"></span>
      <br />
      <b>Text:</b><span data-win-bind="innerText: text"></span>
   </div>
</div>
```

You may have noticed in the previous screenshot that the listed data items contained properties marked with quotes and followed by a colon; for example, `"created_ at":` and `"from_user":`. These properties represent the data that was returned in the `jsonData` object from the web call to Twitter and these properties are passed as parameters to the `data-win-bind` attribute in the `listTemplate` element to be rendered in the DOM.

Next, we should assign this newly created template to the `ListView` control we created earlier, by specifying a value for `itemTemplate` in the `data-win-options` attribute, as shown in the following code:

```
<div id="listViewSample" data-win-control="WinJS.UI.ListView"
data-win-options="{ itemTemplate: select('#listTemplate') }">
</div>
```

Run the project and you will see something similar to the next screenshot. Since live data is being fetched from Twitter, the values will change according to the specific query:

Sorting and filtering the data

We got the data and we used templates to display it and bind it to the `WinJS` control. Now, what if we need to sort the data items or even filter out unwanted items based on a certain criterion? The binding list API provided by the `WinJS` library handles this seamlessly using built-in methods such as `createSorted` and `createFiltered`. If we go back to the code we wrote earlier to fetch the tweets and write the `bindingList` variable we created, which is an instance of `WinJS.Binding.List`, and try to call the method `createSorted`, you will notice the autocomplete feature lists the other two built-in functions provided for this functionality, as shown in the following screenshot:

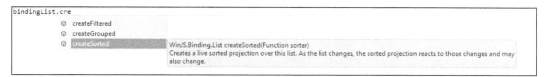

These two methods will create a view over its data called "sorted projection". The `createSorted` method will return a `SortedListProjection` object, which represents a sorted view over the data it holds, and similarly the `createFiltered` method will return a `FilteredListProjection` object representing a filtered view over the data. The main advantage of these two projections is that they are fully observable, which means that when the data in the list changes, its corresponding projection will get a notification and update itself. Additionally, when the projection changes itself, it will notify any listening object about its change.

We can sort this binding list by calling the `createSorted` method, which takes the sorting function parameter that handles the sorting logic. Let's sort the tweets we fetched alphabetically by user name. Use the following code:

```
//to recall this was the bindinglist variable we had
var bindingList = new WinJS.Binding.List(json.results);
//create a sorted list instance from that bindingList
var sortedList = bindingList.createSorted(function (first, second) {
return (first.from_user_name).toString().localeCompare(second.from_
user_name);
});
```

The `createSorted` function will do the sorting logic inside the sorter function parameter that, in this case, compares the `from_user_name` field from the list and returns the list that is sorted alphabetically. Note that the fields to compare are fields from the data items in the list.

Once we are done with the sorting, the `itemDataSource` attribute of the `ListView` control should now bind to the newly created `sortedList` method in order to see the following code:

```
//pass the sortedList as a datasource
simpleListView.itemDataSource = sortedList.dataSource;
```

Build and run the project and you will see a result similar to the following screenshot:

From: Ali
Date: Tue, 07 May 2013 14:30:01 +0000

From: Brandon Casteel
Date: Tue, 07 May 2013 15:03:31 +0000

From: DellHomeUS
Date: Tue, 07 May 2013 15:50:09 +0000

From: J Reid
Date: Tue, 07 May 2013 15:05:23 +0000

From: Jefferson Ramos®
Date: Sun, 05 May 2013 16:28:27 +0000

From: Jefferson Ramos®
Date: Sun, 05 May 2013 15:55:01 +0000

From: Lucas Reis
Date: Sun, 05 May 2013 16:27:16 +0000

From: Marcous Luther
Date: Tue, 07 May 2013 07:52:46 +0000

The filtering is done by calling the `createFiltered` method that creates a live filtered projection over this list. The filtered projection will react to changes in the list and may also change accordingly. This method takes one parameter of type `function`, and what this parameter basically does is execute a callback method on each element in the list. For example, we want to apply a filter to `bindingList` that will check if the `from_user_name` string has the character `'a'` as the second character of its value and return only the matching items in the list. The `createFiltered` parameter of type `function` will check for each string in the list; if the condition returns true, include that string in the filtered list. To use the filter, refer to the following code snippet:

```
//to recall this was the bindinglist variable we had
var bindingList = new WinJS.Binding.List(json.results);//create a
sorted list instance from that bindingList
```

```
var filterdList = bindingList.createFiltered(function (filter) {
return filter.from_user_name.toString().charAt(1) == 'a';
});
simpleListView.itemDataSource = filteredList.dataSource;
```

Run the project and you will see that the list has been filtered accordingly (you can change the filter criteria as you please in order to better see the effect of the filter). The result will be something similar to the following screenshot:

> **From:** Marcous Luther
> **Date:** Tue, 07 May 2013 07:52:46 +0000
>
> **From:** Raphaella
> **Date:** Sun, 05 May 2013 03:24:03 +0000

Summary

In this chapter we have covered the basics for handling data in a JavaScript app. We learned how to get the data from a local object and how to fetch data from the web via a web service and handle the data that is coming back with the response.

We then covered how to display the data we fetched and bind it to a ListView control. Finally, we saw how we can add sorting and filtering to this data before we display it on the app.

In the next chapter we will learn how to make the app responsive to allow the layout to change when the view state changes, so that the content always appears to the user in a good format.

6

Making the App Responsive

In this chapter, we will learn about the different view states that the app can exist in and how we can make the app adapt to these view states and to a variety of form factors and displays sizes. Windows 8 targets different platforms and runs on various devices with dissimilar sizes, from large HD monitors and laptops to 10-inch widescreen tablets and 4-inch-wide smartphones. So, in order to abide by the Windows 8 UX guidelines, the app should maintain the same look and feel and sustain its functionality when users view it on these different devices, they flip their screen to toggle between landscape and portrait orientation, they zoom in or out, or the app switches between the various view states. The app should provide fluid and flexible layouts in a way that allows its UI to reflow gracefully and cater for these changes.

Throughout this chapter, we will learn how to make the app responsive so that it handles screen sizes and view state changes and responds to zooming in and out. We will first introduce the concept of app view states and then we will learn how to handle changes in view states with CSS and JavaScript. Lastly, we will learn about the concept of Semantic Zoom in apps.

Introducing app view states

The view states represent the ways that the user can choose to display the app. There are four possible application view states; they are listed here with the description of each:

- **Full screen landscape view**: With this, the app fills the entire screen, and this is the default state for all Windows Store apps.

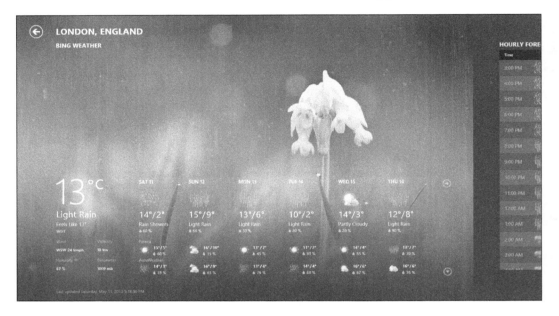

- **Full screen portrait**: With this, the app fills the entire screen again, but this time in a portrait orientation.

- **Snapped view**: With this, the app fills a narrow region of the entire screen (320px) either to the left or right; thus, the screen will display two apps simultaneously.

- **Filled view**: With this, the app runs side by side with a snapped app and it fills the region of the screen that is not occupied by that app; thus, the screen will display two apps simultaneously again.

If we look at the preceding image, we will see two apps running side by side; one in snapped view and the other in filled view. The user has snapped an app (Bing News) by dragging another app (the weather app) or window onto the screen. The second app will become the currently running app and will have the filled view state while the once fullscreen app will be snapped to the side. Now the user can toggle the view state of these apps between snapped and filled by pressing the Windows key and period (.).

Snapping an app resizes it to 320 pixels wide, which allows it to share the screen with another app, thus enabling two apps to be visible at the same time so the user can multitask.

You can have snapped and filled views only on displays with a horizontal resolution greater than or equal to 1366 relative pixels. This is because the snapped view will occupy 320 pixels on either side of the screen. So, the remaining 1046 pixels will be allocated to the splitter (22 pixels) and the app in filled view, which must always have a horizontal resolution of 1024 relative pixels or greater. Thus, the size of 1366 x 768 is considered a reference point.

The app can always be snapped either manually, when the user snaps it to either side, or automatically, in response to another app being dragged into the full screen. Thus, you cannot prevent an app from getting into the snap view. Since users can snap every app, if you don't design your app for the snapped view state, the system will resize your app anyway and might crop the content and mess up the way the app looks.

Rotation, on the other hand, is not obligatory, and you can choose to make your app support it or not. So, if your app does not support portrait orientation and the user flips the device, nothing will happen to your app; that is, it will not rotate with the new device orientation. Having said this, of course, it is highly recommended to support rotation in order to have a satisfied user, who is, after all, the target of your app.

When you click and open the `package_appmanifest` file, you will be able to set up options for the application UI; one of these options is **Supported rotations**, which is an optional setting that indicates the app's orientation preference and has four values: **Landscape**, **Portrait**, **Landscape-flipped**, and **Portrait-flipped**, as shown in the following screenshot:

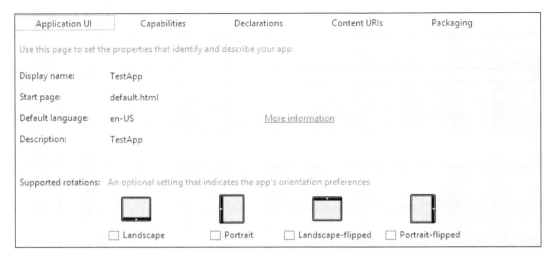

Handling a view state

There are two ways to cater for a snapped view: by using the CSS3 media queries or by using the JavaScript layout change events, and sometimes both. We use media queries for changes in layout that can be tackled using CSS-like element sizes, element display (inline, block), and element visibility. By using CSS media queries, it becomes very easy to define different styles that will be applied depending on the view state of the app. You can use a separate media query for each view state you have, or you can apply the same set of styles to multiple view states by combining more than one media query. The following code shows the syntax for a media query that matches the different view states; the first one matches the snapped view state and the second matches a combination of view states.

```
@media screen and (-ms-view-state: snapped) {
}
@media screen and (-ms-view-state: fullscreen-landscape),
    screen and (-ms-view-state: fullscreen-portrait),
    screen and (-ms-view-state: filled) {
}
```

So, if we have a set of classes and other selectors specifying the styles in the UI, we can change these styles with every media query. For example, the following code shows the wrapper div of the page defined as CSS Grid with two columns; it is changed to a single column layout once inside the media query for the view state snapped:

```
.appGrid {
display: -ms-grid;
-ms-grid-columns: 120px 1fr; /* 2 columns */
-ms-grid-rows: 120px 1fr;
width: 100vw;
height: 100vh;
margin-left: 120px;
}


@media (-ms-view-state: snapped) {
 /*styles that will be applied when in snapped view state*/
   .appGrid {
     display: -ms-grid;
       -ms-grid-columns: 1fr; /* 1 column fills the available space */
     -ms-grid-rows: 120px 1fr;
     width: 100%; height: 100%;
     margin-left: 20px; /* margin decreased from 120 to 20 px*/
 }
 }
```

The units vw and vh, set for the width and height values shown in the preceding code, represent view width and view height respectively, which specify the full width and height resolution that the app is occupying.

The previous code sample shows the use of CSS Grid, which is one of the most convenient ways to achieve a fluid and adaptable UI layout that can handle the change in view states. This is because the Grid automatically expands to distribute the content and fill the available space and it allows you to dictate the position of elements inside it purely by CSS, independent of the order in which they are specified in the HTML markup. This makes it easy to specify the different arrangements for the elements on different screen sizes or in different view states.

The second approach to handling change in window sizes is to use JavaScript events, which are the best option when you tackle changes in behavior and properties that cannot be specified with CSS styles, such as the scroll direction of the `WinJS` ListView control and the control changes (such as changing from a horizontal list of buttons to a drop-down list control). If we take the case of a ListView control, it uses the grid mode to display the items vertically and horizontally in a way that fills the `container` element and the available space when the app is in landscape, is in portrait, or is filled. But when the app is snapped, the ListView control should rearrange and display the items vertically only to avoid horizontal scrolling using the list mode. The list and grid mode cannot be specified in the CSS because they are defined in the `data-win-options` attribute as follows:

```
data-win-options="{ layout: {type: WinJS.UI.GridLayout} }
```

Here is where the JavaScript events come in, allowing us to create view-specific layouts by registering an event listener for the window resize event that queries the `ViewManagement.ApplicationView.value` property, which is provided by the WinRT to directly query the current view state of an app. The following sample shows the code of an event listener for the window resize event:

```
window.addEventListener("resize", function (e) {
    var viewState = Windows.UI.ViewManagement.ApplicationView.value;
    var snapped = Windows.UI.ViewManagement.ApplicationViewState.
snapped;

    if (viewState === snapped) {
        that.listView.layout = new WinJS.UI.ListLayout();
}
    else if (viewState!== snapped)
      {
        that.listView.layout = new WinJS.UI.GridLayout();
}
});
```

ListView and Grid are flexible controls that provide maximum control over the UI with minimum development efforts, as both support the built-in flexible layouts and can arrange and distribute their content automatically. You should try to use them wherever possible.

Understanding semantic zoom

As per the UX guidelines for the Windows Store app, the content flows horizontally and the user will, either by mouse or by touch, scroll the content from left to right or right to left (in some languages). But imagine a scenario where you have content that features a long list of data, such as in the case of an address book or maybe a list of different news articles, where scrolling to navigate the content becomes cumbersome for the user. In the case of an address book app where the contacts are organized alphabetically, the user has to scroll all the way to find a contact whose name starts with the letter z; that is, at the end of list, while the user could zoom out to the view level that only lists the letters and find a specific contact that falls under that letter.

The same goes for a catalog or a news app that organizes items/articles by category; instead of long scrolling to reach the desired content, which falls under a category that happens to be at the end of the list, the user can zoom out to the category level. The following screenshots show a "zoomed-out" view of the People app and Bing News app on Windows 8, respectively:

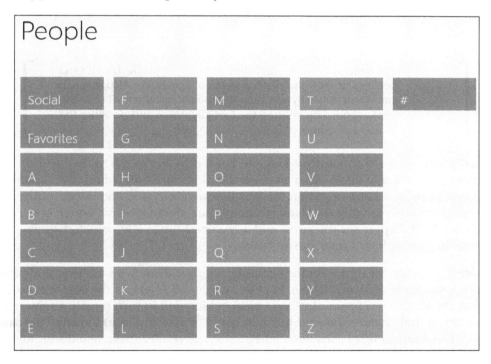

The semantic zoom view of the Bing News app in Windows 8 is shown as follows:

BING NEWS		
FEATURED STORY	TECHNOLOGY AND SCIENCE	ENTERTAINMENT
TOP STORIES	POLITICS	SPORTS
SOURCES	OPINION	
WORLD	BUSINESS	

> The semantic zoom interaction is touch-optimized, so it can be performed with the pinch and stretch gestures. Also, the user can zoom either by scrolling the mouse scroll wheel or using the keyboard by holding the *Ctrl* key down and pressing the plus (+) or minus (-) key.

This technique is called **semantic zoom** and is used by Windows Store apps for presenting—in a single view—two levels of detail for large sets of related content while providing quicker navigation. This technique uses two zoom levels of the same content for organizing the data: a "zoomed-in" detailed view, which is the default mode of display for the apps, and a "zoomed-out" view, which displays the items in groups based on some metadata.

In order to provide the app with the semantic zoom feature, we will need to define these two modes of semantic levels. Luckily, `WinJS.UI` offers us the best way to do so using the `WinJS.UI.SemanticZoom` object, which will in turn render a semantic zoom control that enables the user to zoom between two different views of the same content. The zoom control uses two child controls to render these two different views; the first child control will supply the zoomed-out view and the other will provide the zoomed-in view or vice versa. It is quite easy to declare a semantic zoom control, either in the markup or in script as shown in the following code:

In HTML:

```
<div data-win-control="WinJS.UI.SemanticZoom">
  <!-- zoomed-in view -->
  <!-- zoomed-out view -->
</div>
```

In JavaScript:

```
var object = new WinJS.UI.SemanticZoom(element, options);
```

After we have defined the SemanticZoom control, let's add to it the two child controls that will hold the two views.

Bear in mind that the child controls should support the semantic zoom functionality by implementing the IZoomableView interface, which in turn allows the control to be exposed as either a zoomed-in or a zoomed-out view of the SemanticZoom control. Currently, the only control provided by Windows Library for JavaScript that supports this functionality is the ListView control. Hence, the two child controls will be two instances of a ListView control, as shown in the following code:

```
<!-- zoomed-in view -->
  <div data-win-control="WinJS.UI.SemanticZoom">
    <div id="zoomedInView" data-win-control="WinJS.UI.ListView" >
    </div>

<!-- zoomed-out view -->
    <div id="zoomedOutView" data-win-control="WinJS.UI.ListView">
    </div>
  </div>
```

Now we need some data to display in these two views. Do you recall the data array we created back in *Chapter 4, Developing Apps with JavaScript*, when we were getting introduced to the ListView control? Well, let's use it again and add more names to it. Feel free to add as many as you like; here it is again for reference:

```
var dataArray = [
    { name: "John Doe", country: "England", age: "28" },
    { name: "Jane Doe", country: "England", age: "20" },
    { name: "Mark Wallace", country: "USA", age: "34" },
    { name: "Rami Rain", country: "Lebanon", age: "18" },
    { name: "Ryan Air", country: "England", age: "18" },
    { name: "Foster Mane", country: "England", age: "18" },
    { name: "Doe Jane", country: "England", age: "18" },
```

```
    { name: "Bow Arrow", country: "England", age: "18" },
    { name: "Amy Sparrow", country: "Italy", age: "18" },
    { name: "Jean Trops", country: "France", age: "56" }

    ];
//create a list object from the array
var bindingList = new WinJS.Binding.List(dataArray);
```

Now we need to create a version of this data source that contains the grouping information. We can do so using the createGrouped method, which allows us to create a grouped version of the list. We learned about similar methods, createdFiltered and createSorted, in the previous chapter. The createGrouped method creates a grouped projection over a list and takes the following three function parameters:

- getGroupKey: This takes an item in the list and returns the group key that this item belongs to

- getGroupData: This takes an item in the list and returns the data object that represents the group that this item belongs to

- compareGroups: This compares two groups and returns a negative value if the first group has a lesser value than the second group, zero if the two groups have the same value, and a positive value if the first group has a greater value than the second group

The following code will create a grouped version of our bindingList object, which uses the first letter of each item's name to define the metadata:

```
// Sort the group
function compareGroups(leftKey, rightKey) {
return leftKey.charCodeAt(0) - rightKey.charCodeAt(0);
}

// Get the group key that an item belongs to.
function getGroupKey(dataItem) {
return dataItem.name.toUpperCase().charAt(0);
}

// Get a title for a group
function getGroupData(dataItem) {
return {
    title: dataItem.name.toUpperCase().charAt(0);
};
}
```

```
// Create the groups for the ListView from the item data and the
grouping functions
    var groupedItemsList = bindingList.createGrouped(getGroupKey,
getGroupData, compareGroups);
```

In order to bind the grouped data to the zoomed-out `ListView` control, we set its `itemDataSource` property to `groupedItemsList.groups.dataSource`, which contains the group information, and we set `itemDataSource` for the zoomed-in `ListView` control to `groupedItemsList.dataSource`, which contains the items to display, as follows:

```
var zoomedInView = document.getElementById("zoomedOutView").
winControl;
var zoomedOutView = document.getElementById("zoomedOutView").
winControl;

zoomedInView.itemDataSource = groupedItemsList.dataSource;

zoomedOutView.itemDataSource = groupedItemsList.groups.dataSource;
```

With this knowledge in hand, you can create templates for both views as we learned in *Chapter 4, Developing Apps with JavaScript*, to better present the data.

Summary

In this chapter we got introduced to the different view states that the user can choose to display apps. Then we learned about the techniques and controls that allow us to cater to the changes in these view states, either by CSS and media queries or using JavaScript event handlers that detect the change in window size.

Finally, we learned about semantic zoom and how easy it is to incorporate this feature into an app.

In the following chapter we will learn about live tiles, how to add tiles and badges to the app logo, and make the tiles alive and send notifications from the app to the user.

7
Making the App Live with Tiles and Notifications

The **Start** screen of Windows 8 is flashing with tiles and these tiles are more than just big icons associated with a specific app. In this chapter we will learn about the concept of app tiles, tile types, and the use of each. Also, we will get to see how to define these tiles for the app. Then we will get introduced to notifications and different types of notification methods, and we'll write a sample code that creates and implements a simple notification for the app.

Introducing tiles, badges, and notifications

A unique characteristic of Windows 8 apps is the concept of tiles. Moreover, the tiles are what make a Windows 8 app distinguishable. The apps fill and decorate the **Start** screen with an extravaganza of colors, logos, and information. The tiles are the graphical representation of the app on the **Start** screen. Moreover, an app tile is the launching point of the app; clicking on a tile will start the application similar to what we have with a Windows application shortcut on the desktop.

The following is a screenshot of the **Start** screen from a clean installation that shows a couple of app tiles:

Every installed app has a default tile that is added to the **Start** screen right after installation. This default tile has a default logo image that represents the app logo or any other branding to identify the app. By default, a static content appears on the tile, which contains text specifying the name of the app and an image representing the logo. The previous screenshot shows an example of the basic app tiles on a Windows 8 **Start** screen. You can notice in the previous screenshot that there are two sizes for the tiles: a square (150x150) px and a rectangle (310x150) px. In Windows 8 naming convention, these two sizes are square and wide. As you can see, both sizes display text and images and a notification badge to show some sort of status; we will get to see what a badge is in a bit. All apps support a square tile by default; supporting a wide tile is optional. If an app does not provide a wide logo image for the default tile, users will not be able to make the app tile larger from the **Start** screen menu. Also, if the app includes a wide logo image, Windows 8 will show the tile in its wide format by default.

Users can personalize their **Start** screen by switching between a wide and a square tile as long as the app tile contains both versions. If an app does not contain a wide logo, users will not be able to make the tile larger. Users can right-click on the app and the **Start** screen app bar will appear. From there, users can click on the **Larger** option to change the size of the tile. The following screenshot shows how a user changes the tile of the **Store** app from square to wide.

Windows 8 displays the default tile image as long as it has no notifications to display, and it will revert to the default image when the notification expires or when a user turns off live notifications. Both image sizes and other images such as **Small Logo**, which is displayed in the search results next to the app name, and **Store Logo**, which is displayed on the Windows Store, are included in the app package and are specified in the app manifest under the **Tile Images and Logos** settings in the **Application UI** pane of the Manifest Editor. On the Manifest Editor, we can specify a background color for the tile, the color of the text that will appear on the tile, and a short name for the app; more importantly, we can browse for (and choose images for) the different tile sizes, as shown in the following screenshot:

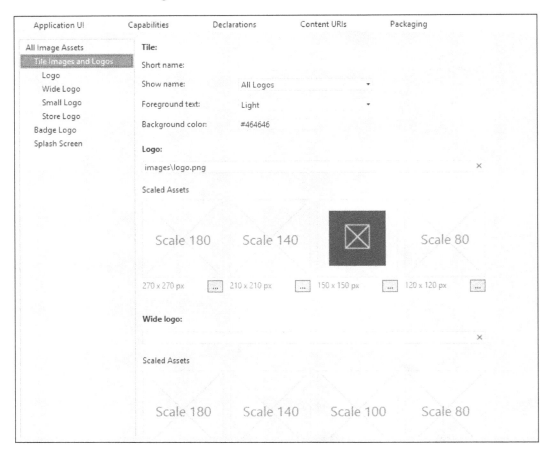

If you check on your **Start** screen for the `test` app we created in the previous chapters, you will see that the app tile displays the image specified in the 150x150 px default logo; it fills the square tile and cannot be made larger. Try choosing a **Wide logo** to run the app, and then make the app tile larger to view the changes. The content of a tile is defined in XML, based on a set of Windows-provided templates, in order to maintain the Windows 8 look and feel. The tile's contents can be defined within these templates by providing the corresponding text or images, or both. The tile also displays either a logo or a short name.

In addition to the default tiles, there are the secondary tiles that enable a user to show specific content from the app on the **Start** screen. The secondary tile is created via the **Pin to Start** option available in the app bar, whereby a user chooses to pin a particular location or content from the app to the **Start** screen. When the app is launched from the secondary tile, the user is directed to a specific location inside that app. For example, we can pin a contact from the **People** app, and the secondary tile will personalize the **Start** screen with the updated info about that contact; alternatively, maybe we can pin the **Weather** of a specific city. Secondary tiles allow the users to personalize their **Start** screen info that is important to them. The following screenshot shows two tiles for the weather app; on the left is the default tile showing the **Weather** from the current location and on the right is the secondary tile showing a pinned content of the weather in the city of **London**:

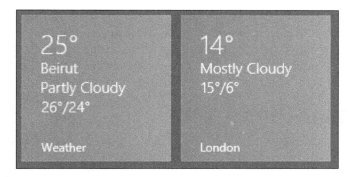

The app tile can convey status information related to the app when it is not running, using a notification badge that expresses a summary or status information that can be numeric between 1 and 99 (values greater than 99 will be displayed as 99+) or it can be a set of Windows-provided image symbols known as **glyphs**. The badges appear on the lower-right corner of the tile and can be featured on both square and wide tiles.

Another UI-related concept of the app is the toast notification; this is a pop-up notification that shows up on the top-right corner of the screen. Toast notifications enable the app to send information to the user when the app is not running on the screen, even if the user is using another app, or when on the desktop and not the Windows 8 **Start** screen.

 It is important to note that app tiles shouldn't be used as an advertisement surface. Using the tile to show ads is not allowed in most cases as per the terms of the Windows Store app.

Working with live tiles

The app tile is a core part of your app; most probably it's the part that is most frequently seen. That is why you should utilize this tile to draw the users' attention and get them back into the app by implementing a live tile. A live tile is one of the ideal ways to attract users to your app by displaying important info that shows the best of what's happening inside the app. For example, the **People** app in Windows 8 has a live tile whereby it changes the pictures of the contacts at specific time intervals.

Unlike a static tile display, for which the default content is generally a full tile logo image and text that indicates the app name, the live tile can update the default tile to show new content. Live tiles can be used to keep the user updated about their contacts, to show event information, or show latest news. Also, a live tile can show a summary of updates in the app, such as the number of unread mails, thus giving users a motive to launch the app.

Sending notifications

Tiles, secondary tiles, lock screen tiles, and toast can be updated through several types of notifications. These notifications can be generated via a local API call or from a call to some service running on the cloud. Additionally, there are four different notification delivery methods that can send tile and badge updates and toast notifications. These methods include the following:

- **Local**: It sends notifications while the app is running either on the screen or in the background to update an app tile or badge, or pops up a toast notification.
- **Scheduled**: It sends a notification at a certain time that is known in advance; for example, a reminder for an upcoming appointment.

- **Periodic**: It sends notifications in a periodic manner by polling for new content from a cloud server at fixed time intervals; for example, updating the weather every 12 hours. Periodic notifications work with tiles and badges but are not suitable for toasts.

- **Push**: It sends notifications from a cloud server directly to the screen even if the app is not running. Push notifications are ideal for situations that include real-time data such as social network updates or time-sensitive information such as instant message or breaking news. This notification method can be used with tiles, badges, and toast.

By default, local tile notifications do not expire but can be and ideally should be given an expiration time; push, periodic, and scheduled notifications, however, expire after three days from the time when they were provided. By specifying an expiration time, the app can remove the notification content from the tile if it is still being displayed when it hits the expiry time.

Choosing a notification method is determined primarily by the information that you want to deliver and the nature and content of the app.

 Bear in mind that a user can turn tile notifications off and on at any time, so be wary of overwhelming the user with unnecessary toast notifications.

In order to implement the notifications feature and allow the app to transmit toast notifications, we must declare it as toast capable in the manifest file. Once the app has been declared toast capable, it will be added to the list of apps in the **Notifications:** section of the **PC** settings. The following screenshot shows where to change the **Toast capable** setting:

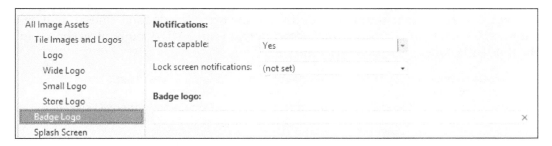

Now let's write some code to create a simple local toast notification. We will need to use the `Windows.UI.Notifications` namespace very frequently; so, for the purpose of simplicity let's declare a namespace variable as follows:

```
var notifications = Windows.UI.Notifications;
```

Next, we need to provide a `ToastTemplateType` by choosing from one of the Windows-provided templates; these templates ensure that an app will maintain the expected Windows 8 look and feel in the toast notifications. There are text templates such as: **toastText01, toastText02, toastText03, toastText04**. The templates for image and text are: **toastImageAndText01, toastImageAndText02, toastImageAndText03, toastImageAndText04**.

`WinJS` provides IntelliSense for these templates, which will be listed when we call the `ToastTemplateType` enumeration on the notifications variable, as shown in the following screenshot:

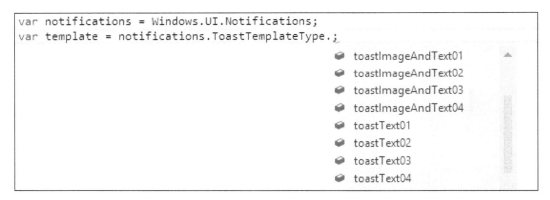

For this example, we'll choose the `toastText01` that contains only a single text string that wraps across a maximum of three lines. If the text exceeds three lines, it will be truncated. We'll then get the template content that is an XML document as shown in the following code:

```
var template = notifications.ToastTemplateType.toastText01;
var templateXML =
notifications.ToastNotificationManager.getTemplateContent(template
);
```

The `templateContent` variable will contain the following XML skeleton:

```
<toast>
  <visual>
    <binding template="toastText01">
```

```
      <text id="1"> </text>
    </binding>
  </visual>
</toast>
```

The next thing we need to do is fill the content in this XML template, so we need to retrieve the element with a tag name `text`, as shown in the following code:

```
var toastTextElements =
  templateContent.getElementsByTagName("text");
toastTextElements[0].appendChild(templateXML.createTextNode("This
  is a new toast notification"));
```

Then we create the toast notification based on the XML content we've just specified, as follows:

```
var newToast = new notifications.ToastNotification(templateXML);
```

Lastly, we will create a `toastNotifier` variable which will send `newToast`, the toast notification we defined to the screen, as shown in the following code:

```
var toastNotifier = notifications.ToastNotificationManager.
createToastNotifier();
toastNotifier.show(newToast);
```

Write the code to be executed in the `then()` function called on the `WinJS.UI.processAll()` method; thus the toast notification will appear as soon as the app starts. If we run the app now, the following toast notification will pop up in the top-right corner of the screen:

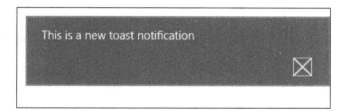

 Note that the background color applied to the toast notification is the one declared in the app manifest for the app's tile.

The previous code allowed us to implement a minimal toast notification; you can experiment with the rest of the toast templates and compare the results.

Summary

In this chapter we got introduced to the concept of tiles, badges, and notifications at the UI level, and we learned the difference between each of them and where we can use them.

We also learned how to send notifications and wrote a sample code which implements sending a very simple toast notification to the screen.

In the next chapter, we will learn how to use the Windows Live Services to enable user authentication and allow the users to sign in using their e-mail IDs.

8
Signing Users in

A Windows Store app can be personalized for users who sign in to the app; thus, it is fairly important to make the authentication process very simple. Windows 8 enables users to sign in to their devices by using a Microsoft account, hence making it easier for developers to provide a single sign-on experience for users on their apps. Furthermore, Windows 8 offers a **Software Development Kit (SDK)** and a set of APIs to allow Windows Store apps to enable single sign on with Microsoft accounts, and to integrate with info in Microsoft SkyDrive, Outlook.com, and Windows Live Messenger. In this chapter we will learn about the Live Connect API and how to integrate the apps with this API to sign in users and retrieve user profile information. We will learn how to start integrating the apps with Live Connect, and show some code that introduces a few basic things that the Live Connect APIs can do.

Introducing Live Connect

There are many scenarios when an app will need to authenticate users and access their profile info, from the simple purpose of displaying a welcome message with a user's name to the extent of accessing their profile info and giving the user a personalized experience. Moreover, you can build an app that offers great features by integrating with products and services such as Microsoft SkyDrive that allows working with documents and media and accessing files on the cloud or Outlook to work with contacts and calendars. The scenarios where your app will need to integrate authentication with Microsoft accounts can be summed up as follows:

- The app requires the user to be signed in to work, for example, a contacts app
- The app can work without needing the user to sign in but delivers a more personalized experience for those who do; for example, a weather or news app
- The app contains certain features that integrate with SkyDrive or Hotmail, and thus require a Microsoft account sign in

The authentication process and the integration with Microsoft cloud services such as Microsoft SkyDrive and Outlook are implemented using Live Connect. Live Connect is a set of APIs that allow integrating the app with these compatible services. These APIs are provided by the Live SDK that is one of the Microsoft Software Development kits for developing apps. The Live Connect APIs utilize an open standard that allows you to focus on coding to implement features, rather than spending time learning new concepts when all you want to do is implement the features introduced by this new concept. For example, you can use the **Open Authentication (OAuth)** standard to integrate with the authentications services of Facebook and other social networking APIs without having to learn the internal workings of the authentication process at the level of those social networking APIs; more importantly, you can use the programming language you know to do the calls. The open standards used by Live Connect include the following:

- **OAuth 2.0**: It is the latest version of the OAuth protocol that is an open standard for authenticating users' credentials. Social networking APIs, including Live Connect, have adopted OAuth as its authentication standard. OAuth basically enables users to be authenticated using the Live Connect authorization web services without having to share their confidential sign-in credentials with the apps.

- **Representational State Transfer (REST)**: It is an architectural style popular in web services implementation. In Windows Store development, REST allows us to easily request users' info through Live Connect APIs. This REST implementation supports standard HTTP methods such as GET, PUT, POST, and DELETE.

- **JSON**: It stands for **JavaScript Object Notation**, a lightweight data-interchange format used for representing info in web services. Live Connect exchanges user info in JSON format. For instance, when the function requests a user's profile information, that info is returned in a response object that contains `first_name`, `last_name`, and so on.

In Windows 8, users can sign in to their devices by using their Microsoft accounts (Hotmail, Live, and Outlook); hence, the app can take advantage of this functionality to provide a single sign-on experience. For example, the main apps of Windows 8 such as People, Mail, and Messaging, and also Microsoft websites such as Outlook and Bing can take advantage of the single sign-on, so the users don't need to sign in to these apps and websites after they are signed into the PC; the process will be done on their behalf. The apps we develop can do the same by implementing the features in the Live Connect APIs so that a user can be directly authenticated in our apps if already signed in to the device.

Before we can start using Live Connect features, there are two prerequisites:

- Register the app with the Windows Store
- Configure the Live Connect settings for the Windows Store apps in your Windows Store Dashboard

First we need to register the app on the Store in your Windows Store Dashboard, which can be accessed via the following link:

```
https://appdev.microsoft.com/StorePortals/en-us/Home/Index
```

Sign in to the store dashboard; you will need Microsoft account credentials for that, and you will see the following screen:

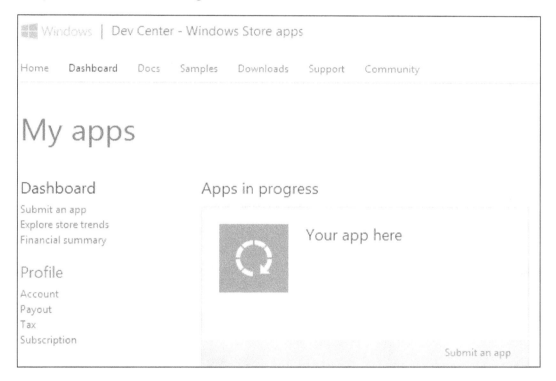

This is the main page where your entire app will be listed. Also, this is the screen that the first-time users will see. In order for the app to start using the Live Connect APIs, it must be registered and its settings configured accordingly. Additionally, for a Windows Store app to use Live Connect, it will need to have a package identity that is a combination of a package name and publisher and that will uniquely identify the app. To get the package identity, we need to submit the app; this is basically reserving a name for your app, adding its description, and submitting it for certification. At this level, we don't need to submit the app to the Windows Store for certification; we will just need to enter a name for it in the Windows Store developer account. In order to do so, we'll start by clicking on the **Submit an app** link, which is the first link in the menu to the left under **Dashboard**, as you may have noticed in the previous screenshot. You will be directed to the **Submit an app** page, as shown in the following screenshot:

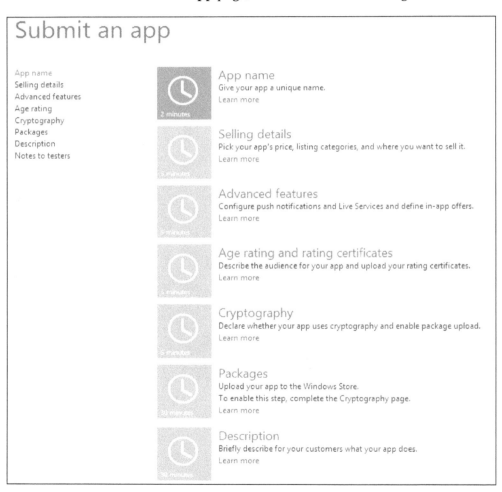

Click on **App name** to give the app a unique name that will be reserved for this app only; no other app can use it. The reservations will last for one year if the app was not fully submitted to the Store. Make sure that you have the rights to use the name because the app will be listed in the Windows Store under this name. Note that the app name should be the same as the one entered for the **DisplayName** field in the app manifest file. To proceed, enter a value in the text box provided and click on **Reserve app name**; the name is now reserved; click on **Save** to return to the app summary page. Now the app will be listed on the dashboard in a tilelike box containing **Delete** and **Edit** links. The following screenshot shows a test app created to serve as an example:

Next we need to configure the Live Services for the app. To do so, follow the given steps:

1. If you are in the dashboard page, locate your app and click on **Edit**. You will be directed to the app summary page.

2. Click on **Advanced features**.

3. Click on **Push Notifications and Live Connect services info**.

4. You will be directed to the page **Push notifications and Live Connect services info page** and will need to follow the steps under the heading **If your app uses Live Connect services, review**. It includes the following steps:

   ○ Identifying your app

This includes defining the correct identity values in the app's manifest. These values have been created when we reserved an app name. We can set these values in two ways:

1. We could set the app's identity values by using the **Store** menu in Visual Studio 2012 for Windows 8. Within an open project, in the top menu, click on **Project**; then select **Store** from the menu that appears, navigate to the submenu, and click on **Associate App with the Store**. Follow and finish the wizard, the process is illustrated in the following screenshot:

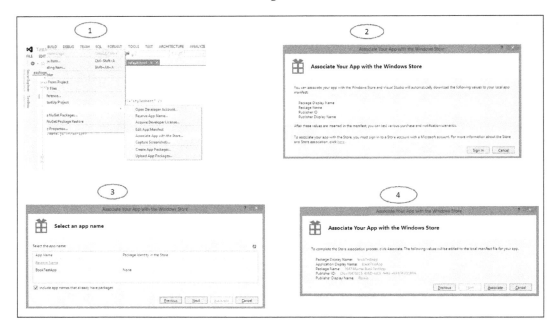

In the first step of the wizard, marked by number 2 in the previous screenshot, you will be prompted to sign in using your Microsoft account.

2. Alternatively, we can set the app's package identity manually in the app manifest file. Open your app's `AppManifest.xml` file in a text editor and set these attributes of the `<identity>` element using the `Name` and `Publisher` values. The Windows Store created these values when you reserved your app's name, and you can retrieve it from the Windows Store Dashboard. The following code shows the syntax of the XML setting node that contains these values:

```
<Identity Name="19474XXX.BookTestApp" Publisher="CN=F0476225-496D-
4EDF-946E-46F6247D5B9A"" />
```

     °   Authenticating your service

This step involves retrieving the client secret values. Live Connect services use the client secret to authenticate the communications from your server in order to protect your app's security. The following client secret will be displayed:

zqMKo4G0t3ICZe1h06ofrKYZ1/hVuZXn.

Note that you can always come back to the page and create a new client secret if there is a need.

     °   Representing your app to Live Connect users

This is the last step to configure the Live Connect services info and involves specifying the settings for the consent dialog that Live Connect services use to prompt the user for permission to access and interact with their data. In this step, you can provide them with the links to your own terms of service and privacy policy, and upload your app logo to be displayed in the consent dialog.

That concludes the registration and configuration process of the app on the Windows Store. Now to the coding part; we'll see how to enable a basic sign-in and authentication functionality.

Signing in users to the app

To start coding the sign-in functionality, we need to reference the Live Connect APIs in our app solution; in order to do so, we should first download and install Live SDK for Windows if you haven't already installed it. It can be found and downloaded from the *Live Connect Developer Center* via the following link:

```
http://msdn.microsoft.com/en-us/live/ff621310.aspx
```

On that page, you will also find download links to Live SDK versions that support Android and iOS. Alternatively, you can find and install Live SDK in Visual Studio directly to your open solution using the NuGet Package Manager.

To do so, open the app solution in Visual Studio, right-click on the solution from the **Solution Explorer**, and click on **Manage NuGet Packages...**

A dialog will appear, type `livesdk` in the search textbox provided at the top right of the dialog; the package manager will search online for all the relevant matches that include `livesdk`. From the search results, locate **Live SDK** and click on **Install**. This will install the Live SDK package and include it in the references.

The following screenshot shows the **Manage NuGet Packages** dialog on the screen:

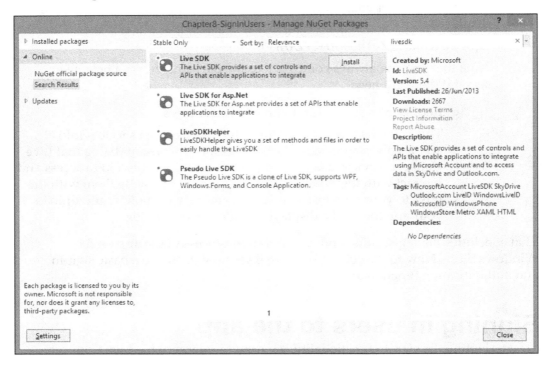

Next, we add a reference to the Live Connect APIs in our project. For doing so, follow the given steps:

1. From the **Solution Explorer**, right-click on **References** and then click on **Add Reference**.
2. Click on **Windows | Extension SDKs | Live SDK**.
3. Click on **Add** and then click on **Close**.

Once we add the reference to the Live SDK, the JavaScript file `wl.js` will be added to the solution. For convenience, I recommend you to copy and paste this file to your `js` folder. Then we add the `<script>` element that points to the newly added `wl.js`, so we can make use of the Microsoft IntelliSense for this API in `default.html` pages, as shown in the following code:

```
<script src="///LiveSDKHTML/js/wl.js"></script>
```

Notice that the file path set for the `src` attribute contains `///`; the reason we used 3 backslashes (`/`) was because there are three levels in the directory hierarchy to reach the `wl.js` file that is located in the directory `js` under `LiveSDKHTML` under `References`.

Adding the reference to this script file will enable Microsoft IntelliSense in the HTML file it is being referenced in.

Moreover, if you want to enable the intelliSense at the level of JavaScript, add the reference to the top of the JavaScript file you are using to call methods of this API, as shown in the following code:

```
/// <reference path="///LiveSDKHTML/js/wl.js" />
```

 It is recommended you write the code that uses the `wl.js` in a separate JavaScript file. This will make it easier to make modifications and debug the app.

Let's add a button that when clicked, will prompt the user to sign in and respond to the consent dialog.

The following markup will add a `button` with ID `signIn` and a `div` with ID `log`. This `div` will be used to display content on the screen that will give us an idea of what is happening when we click on the **Sign in** button:

```
<div id="liveSDK">
  <h1>Windows Live Connect</h1>
<div>
<div>
  The authentication in this section uses the Windows Live connect.
  <br />
  Sign in to your Microsoft account by clicking on the below button:
</div>
<button id="signIn">Sign in</button><br /><br />
<div id="log"><br /></div>
</div>
</div>
```

First we initialize the Live Connect APIs by calling the `WL.init` method (the app must call this function on every page before making other function calls in the library), and then subscribe to the `auth.login` event on the page load, as shown in the following code:

```
WL.init();
WL.Event.subscribe("auth.login", function () {
  if (WL.getSession()){
    log("You are now signed in!");
  }
});
```

On the callback function of the `auth.login` event, we check the status using the `WL.getSession()` method that gets the current session object; if it exists, the user is signed in.

Next, we will add the sign-in functionality on the click of the button and the log function:

```
document.querySelector("#signIn").onclick = function (e) {
  if (WL.getSession()){
    log("You are already signed in!");
}
  else {
    WL.login({ scope: "wl.signin" });
  }
};
//log what is happening
function log(info) {
  var message = document.createTextNode(info);
  var logDiv = document.querySelector("#log");
  logDiv.appendChild(message);
  logDiv.appendChild(document.createElement("br"));
}
```

On the click of the sign in button, we first check if there is a session and whether the user is signed in already. If there is no session, we attempt to log in the user by calling the `WL.login` method; this method takes the parameter `scope: "wl.signin"`. The scope values such as `"wl.signin"` or `"wl.skydrive"` are used to indicate what parts of the user data the app will be able to access if the user consents.

In the previous lines of code, we defined a single scope using this format: `scope: "wl.signin"`, which is a string parameter. We can define multiple scopes as well, but with a slightly different format, using an array of string values, as shown in the following line of code:

```
scope: ["wl.signin", "wl.skydrive", "wl.basics"]
```

The scope can also be set when initializing the library by passing it as an optional parameter to the `WL.init` method. Moreover, the scope values entered in the `login` method will override and extend the list of scopes defined in the `init` method. Also, the scope value of `WL.init` is used when there was no scope provided by the `login` method.

The `WL.login` function should be called only in response to a user action, such as clicking a button as in our example, because this function can result in launching the consent page prompt.

The `log` function only takes text, and simply appends it to the contents of the `div` with the ID `log` so that we can get status info of what has happened.

Run the app now. You will see the following screenshot prompting you to log in; the consent dialog will follow:

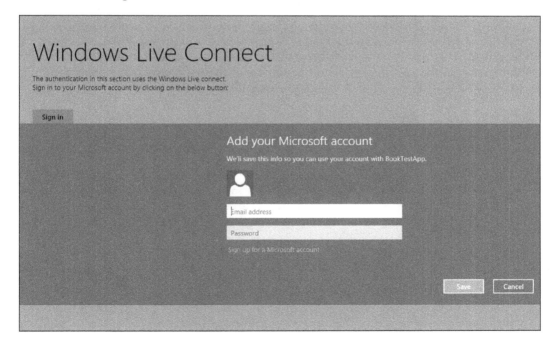

Follow the steps that appear in the previous screenshot. At the end, the app will display the message: **You are signed in!**

Getting user info

The `login` function returns a promise object that allows us to properly react in case of a success, that is, a successful sign-in by the user. Our goal is to get the user's profile information. As such we need to modify the previously shown `WL.login` call and request additional scopes such as `wl.basic`, `wl.birthday`, and `wl.emails`, which will allow us to retrieve basic profile information such as first and last names and also get the user's birthday and e-mails. In the success callback of the login method, we then execute a call to the `WL.api` function, which returns our desired user profile info. Technically, the `WL.api` function makes a call to the Live Connect Representational State Transfer (REST) API. The syntax to the `WL.api` call is shown in the following code:

```
WL.api({
    path: "me" ,
    method: "GET"
});
```

In the previous code sample, we passed the `me` shortcut to request info about the signed-in user. The path parameter specifies the path to the REST API object, in this case the object `me`, which contains properties such as `first_name` and `last_name`; `WL.api` returns a promise object so we can call `then()` on it, and in the success callback we will request the first and last names of the user, which are provided by the scope `"wl.basic"`. The code will be as follows:

```
WL.api({
  path: "me" , method: "GET"
  }).then(
  function (response) {
    log("First Name: " + response.first_name);
    log("Last Name: " + response.last_name);
    log("Email: " + response.emails.preferred);
    log("Birthday: " + response.birth_day + "/" +
      response.birth_month);
}
```

Add the previous code to the `then` method called on `WL.login` in the sign-in button click handler, and the complete code will be as follows:

```
document.querySelector("#signIn").onclick = function (e) {
  WL.login({
```

```
    scope: ["wl.signin", "wl.basic", "wl.birthday", "wl.emails"]
}).then(
function (response) {
  WL.api({
      path: "me", method: "GET"
      }).then(
      function (response) {
        log("First Name: " + response.first_name);
        log("Last Name: " + response.last_name);
        log("Emails: " + response.emails.preferred);
        log("Birthday: " + response.birth_day + "/" +
          response.birth_month);
        }
      );
    }
  );
};
```

Run the app now and you will notice that the consent dialog will change requesting to access to info about your birthday and e-mail address, as shown in the following screenshot:

After you approve the consent prompt, click on the **Sign in** button and the app will display the requested info, as shown in the following screenshot:

Windows Live Connect

The authentication in this section uses the Windows Live connect.
Sign in to your Microsoft account by clicking on the below button:

Sign in

First Name: Rami
Last Name: Sarieddine
Emails: r.sarieddine@live.com
Birthday: 5/6

> To abide by the guidelines set by Microsoft for the Windows Store apps, you should not display the Microsoft account sign-in or sign-out options anywhere on the app other than the **Settings Flyout** control or part of a task. The users expect account management options to be in the Settings charm and changing its location will lead to an inconsistent and unexpected experience for your users.

Summary

In this chapter, we were introduced to Live Connect and learned about its core concepts and saw what we can do with these APIs, what settings are needed by the app to start calling the APIs, and how to write the basic code to call the APIs.

We also covered how to register the app on the Store and communicate with the Store from within Visual Studio.

Then we got to utilize the Live Connect APIs and sign in the user to the app. Also, we learned how to get session info after the user signs consent.

In the next chapter we will learn about the app bar, how to create one for the app, and how to add menu buttons to it.

9

Adding Menus and Commands

In this chapter we will learn about the app bar and understand how it works and where it is found on the app. Moreover, we will cover how to declare an app bar and add controls to it.

Understanding the app bar

When you run a Windows Store app, all you see is a full screen app that allows you to be immersed in the content of the app; however, then you ask yourself where all the buttons and controls are. They are all contained and hidden in the app bar—hidden till you need them, of course—to avoid distractions and make use of every pixel on the screen for the content of the app.

The app bar can be found at the bottom of the screen and appears when triggered by the user. This can be done with a touch gesture (by tapping or swiping upward from the bottom edge or downward from the top edge), using the mouse (by right-clicking), or using the keyboard (via the shortcut Windows + Z). The app bar typically holds the controls that are relevant to the current screen. By default, the controls are equally split between the left-hand and right-hand side of the screen. The left-hand side contains the commands that are specific to the content that is currently being shown in the app and the right-hand side holds the commands that are global to the app and apply to all the pages. The app bar can also contain commands that are specific to a single element in the app.

Let's have a look at a sample app bar. The following screenshot shows the app bar of the Microsoft Bing app that contains four commands, namely **Copy Link**, **Copy**, **Save As**, and **Set As Lock Screen**:

The app bar's hiding mechanism allows users to focus and get immersed in the content and minimizes distractions. It provides the user with consistent and easy access to the commands when they need them, and they can easily see or hide the app bar.

When we try to show the app bar using the mouse, touch, or keyboard, another bar will appear simultaneously located at the top of the screen. This is the navigation bar and though it may look similar, it is not an app bar. The navigation bar is used to show controls that help us navigate between different sections of an application.

The app bar, if it exists, should always be available to the user and thus adapt to changes in the layout between snapped and portrait views. For example, if you can't fit all the commands in a snapped view, you can try to group them into menus and provide tooltips for the commands, even though Windows will automatically hide the labels and adjust the padding accordingly.

 It is strongly recommended that you do not change the size or the padding of buttons that are applied by the default layout provided by WinJS, since it is designed to fit 10 commands on all supported screen sizes; more importantly, it is designed to support touch gestures. Hence, making changes to the layout may disrupt this behavior.

The app bar is made available by the WinJS library using the object WinJS.UI.AppBar.

It is very trivial to declare an app bar in the markup. We start by creating an app bar from a simple div element by simply specifying a WinJS.UI.AppBar control in the data-win-control attribute. The syntax will be as follows:

```
<div id="testAppBar" data-win-control="WinJS.UI.AppBar"> </div>
```

The preceding syntax will create an empty app bar that will be displayed when triggered either by a mouse or an upward swipe.

The app bar is made to contain command buttons, so let's add a command button inside the app bar. In order to create an app bar command button, we will use a button element and specify its data-win-control attribute to be AppBarCommand, as shown in the following code:

```
<div id="testAppBar" data-win-control="WinJS.UI.AppBar">
  <button data-win-control="WinJS.UI.AppBarCommand"></button>
</div>
```

The preceding syntax will show the app with an empty command button inside. We can add life to this command button by specifying some options in the data-win-options attribute. These options are as follows:

- type: This option indicates the type of command from the following values – button, toggle, separator, and flyout.
- Id: This option specifies an ID for the command.
- label: This option specifies the text to be displayed on the app bar.

- `Icon`: This option specifies an icon to be displayed for the command either by choosing a value from the `AppBarIcon` list provided by Windows, such as `pin`, `unpin`, `accept`, `cancel`, and `delete`, or by specifying the path to a custom PNG image file.

- `section`: This option indicates the section to which the command belongs, either `selection` or `global`. The `selection` section will place the command to the left of the app bar, which is reserved for contextual or page-specific commands, while the `global` section will place the command to the right, which is reserved for global or app-level commands.

- `tooltip`: This option specifies an info tooltip (hint) to be displayed when the user hovers over the command.

The following code shows what the syntax will look like after adding these options for the command button that we declared in the previous example:

```
<button data-win-control="WinJS.UI.AppBarCommand"
data-win-options="{type:'button', id:'testCmd', label:'Test Command',
icon:'placeholder', section:'global', tooltip: 'Command Tooltip' }">
</button>
```

Run the app and you will see an app bar.as shown in the following screenshot:

As you can see in the preceding screenshot, the app bar contains a button that has the placeholder icon, labeled as **Test Command**; when hovered over, it will display the tooltip **Command Tooltip**.

Adding functionality to the commands

The app bar we just created doesn't really do anything yet, so let's add another command and check the other types. But before that, we need a separator between the two commands; it can be created using an `hr` element that the app bar contains by default in addition to the command buttons.

The `hr` element will also need to have the `data-win-control="WinJS.UI.AppBarCommand"` attribute set on it. The syntax for creating a separator will look like the following code:

```
<hr data-win-control="WinJS.UI.AppBarCommand"
  data-win-options="{type:'separator', section:'global'}" />
```

After the separator, we'll add a new button command but this time we will choose the pin icon; the syntax will look as follows:

```
<div id="testAppBar" data-win-control="WinJS.UI.AppBar">
<button data-win-control="WinJS.UI.AppBarCommand"
  data-win-options="{ type:'button', id:'pinCmd', label:'Pin to
  start', icon:'pin', section:'global', tooltip: 'Pin the app'}">
</button>
<hr data-win-control="WinJS.UI.AppBarCommand"
  data-win-options="{type:'separator', section:'global'}" />
<button data-win-control="WinJS.UI.AppBarCommand"
  data-win-options="{type:'button', id:'testCmd', label:'Test
  Command', icon:'placeholder', section:'global', tooltip:
  'Command Tooltip' }">
</button>
</div>
```

Run the app now and you should see two command buttons, one with a pin icon and the other with a placeholder icon, and a separator between these two that looks like an `hr` element. The following is the screenshot of the resulting app bar when the user hovers over the command labeled **Pin to start**:

These commands look nice on the app bar but still do nothing when clicked on, so let's add some functionality to the **Pin to start** command button and start the app pin.

To add some functionality to the command buttons, we need to retrieve them from the app bar and add to it a `click` event handler. The following code gets the app bar and sets it to a variable. Then, it gets the specific command in that app bar using its `Id` attribute and attaches a function to its click event:

```
//get the appbar control
var appbar = document.getElementById("testAppBar").winControl;
//get the command and add an event handler to it
appbar.getCommandById("pinCmd").addEventListener("click", clickPin,
false);
//function to be called when the command is clicked
function clickPin() {
var dialog = new Windows.UI.Popups.MessageDialog("The pin command in
the bar has been clicked.");
dialog.showAsync();
}
```

Run the app now and click on the **Pin to start** command button; a pop-up message dialog will appear on the screen.

The app bar is by default located at the bottom of the app and can be changed to be at the top of the screen; however, it should contain navigational elements that move the user to a different page. The top app bar, according to the Windows 8 UX guidelines, is a navigational bar. Getting back to the code, we can change the location of the app bar from the bottom to the top by simply setting the value of the `placement` property of the `data-win-options` attribute in the app bar control, as shown in the following code:

```
<div id="testAppBar" data-win-control="WinJS.UI.AppBar"
  data-win-options="{placement:'top'}">
```

But again, the default and recommended behavior by the UX guidelines is to place the app bar at the bottom, since the top bar is reserved for navigational commands.

In the previous examples, we have added the app bar to the main page, `default.html`, but in fact the page we should choose to include our app bar in is not arbitrary and depends on its scope, as follows:

- Add the app bar to the `default.html` page if it contains commands that are global and should be available to all the pages
- Add the app bar to a specific page (a `PageControl` object) if it contains commands that are specific to one page and will differ between a page and another

Alternatively, we can define a default app bar in the main `default.html` file and then do the required modifications on the app bar on the load event of that particular page, which requires different commands from the default.

Summary

In this chapter, we saw what app bars are and where we can place the commands and controls for the app. We also learned about the difference between an app bar and a navigational bar. We saw what app bar commands are and the different options they can hold. Then we saw how to create a simple app bar containing commands and separators.

Finally, we saw how to add basic functionality to any command type on the app bar.

In the next chapter we will reach the final destination of a Windows Store app; that is, submitting to the Store itself, and we will learn how to publish the app to the Store from Visual Studio and handle the app configuration on the dashboard.

10
Packaging and Publishing

Windows Store is like a huge shopping mall and your app, once published to the Store, will be like a small shop in that mall; the Windows Store Dashboard is where you will set all the branding, advertising, and marketing material for the shop. Visual Studio is your production environment and the Store is your destination, and everything else in between is in the Windows Store Dashboard. In this chapter we will be introduced to the Store and learn how to get an app through all the stages into publishing. Also, we will see how we can interact with the Store from within Visual Studio.

Introducing the Windows Store

Developing a Windows Store app is not just about design, coding, and markup. A very essential part of the process that leads to a successful app is done on the Windows Store Dashboard. It is the place where you submit the app, pave its way to the market, and monitor how it is doing there. Also, it is the place where you can get all the information about your existing apps and where you can plan your next app. We already had a sneak preview of the Dashboard in *Chapter 8, Signing Users in*, when we were learning how to add authentication and the sign-in functionality. The submission process is broken down into seven phases, and in *Chapter 8, Signing Users in*, we completed the first step in the Release Summary page, which is reserving an app name and registering the app with Windows Store. There are six more steps to complete in order to submit the app for certification. If you haven't already opened a Windows Store developer account, now is the time to do so because you will need it to access your Dashboard. Before you sign up, make sure you have a credit card. The Windows Store requires a credit card to open a developer account even if you had a registration code that entitles you to a free registration.

Once signed in, locate your app listed on the home page under the **Apps in progress** section and click on **Edit**. This will direct you to the Release Summary page and the app will be titled **AppName: Release 1**. The release number will auto-increment each time you submit a new release for the same app. The Release Summary page lists the steps that will get your app ready for Windows Store certification. On this page, you can enter all the info about your Windows Store app and upload its packages for certification. At the moment you will notice that the two buttons at the bottom of the page labeled as **Review release info** and **Submit app for certification** are disabled and will remain so until all the previous steps have been marked **Complete**. The submission progress can always be saved to be resumed later, so it is not necessarily a one-time mission. We'll go over these steps one by one:

1. **App name**: This is the first step and it includes reserving a unique name for the app.

2. **Selling details**: This step includes selecting the following:
    ° The **app price tier** option sets the price of your app (for example, free or 1.99 USD).

    ° The **free trial period** option is the number of days the customer can use the app before they start paying to use it. This option is enabled only if the **app price tier** is not set to **Free**.

    ° The **Market** where you would like the app to be listed in the Windows Store. Bear in mind that if your app isn't free, your developer account must have a valid tax profile for each country/region you select.

    ° The **release date** option specifies the earliest date when the app will be listed in the Windows Store. The default option is to release as soon as the app passes the certification.

    ° The **App category and subcategory** option indicates where your app be listed in the Store, which in turn lists the apps under **Categories**.

    ° The **Hardware requirements** option will specify the minimum requirements for the DirectX feature level and the system RAM.

    ° The **Accessibility** option is a checkbox that when checked indicates that the app has been tested to meet accessibility guidelines.

3. **Services**: In this step, you can add services to your app such as Windows Azure Mobile Services and Live Services (just as we did in *Chapter 8, Signing Users in*). You can also provide products and features that the customer can buy from within the app called In-app offers.

4. **Age rating and rating certificates**: In this step, you can set an age rating for the app from the available Windows Store age ratings. Also, you can upload country/region-specific rating certificates in case your app is a game.

5. **Cryptography**: In this step, you specify if your app calls, supports, and contains or uses cryptography or encryption. The following are some of the examples of how an app might apply cryptography or encryption:

   ° Use of a digital signature such as authentication or integrity checking

   ° Encryption of any data or files that your app uses or accesses

   ° Key management, certificate management, or anything that interacts with a public key infrastructure

   ° Using a secure communication channel such as NTLM, Kerberos, **Secure Sockets Layer (SSL)**, or **Transport Layer Security (TLS)**

   ° Encrypting passwords or other forms of information security

   ° Copy protection or **digital rights management (DRM)**

   ° Antivirus protection

6. **Packages**: In this step, you can upload your app to the Store by uploading the `.appxupload` file that was created in Visual Studio during the package-creation process. We will shortly see how to create an app package. The latest upload will show on the Release Summary page in the packages box and should be labeled as **Validation Complete**.

7. **Description**: In this step you can add a brief description (mandatory) on what the app does for your customers. The description has a 10,000-character limit and will be displayed in the **details** page of the app's listing in the Windows Store. Besides description, this step contains the following features:

   ° **App features**: This feature is optional. It allows you to list up to 20 of the app's key features.

   ° **Screenshots**: This feature is mandatory and requires to provide at least one `.png` file image; the first can be a graphic that represents your app but all the other images must be screenshots with a caption taken directly from the app.

   ° **Notes**: This feature is optional. Enter any other info that you think your customer needs to know; for example, changes in an update.

   ° **Recommended hardware**: This feature is optional. List the hardware configurations that the app will need to run.

   ° **Keywords**: This feature is optional. Enter keywords related to the app to help its listing appear in search results.

- **Copyright and trademark info**: This feature is mandatory. Enter the copyright and trademark info that will be displayed to customers in the app's listing page.

- **Additional license terms**: This feature is optional. Enter any changes to the **Standard App License Terms** that the customers accept when they acquire this app.

- **Promotional images**: This feature is optional. Add images that the editors use to feature apps in the Store.

- **Website**: This feature is optional. Enter the URL of the web page that describes the app, if any.

- **Support contact info**: This feature is mandatory. Enter the support contact e-mail address or URL of the web page where your customers can reach out for help.

- **Privacy policy**: This feature is optional. Enter the URL of the web page that contains the privacy policy.

8. **Notes to testers**: This is the last step and it includes adding notes about this specific release for those who will review your app from the Windows Store team. The info will help the testers understand and use this app in order to complete their testing quickly and certify the app for the Windows Store.

Each step will remain disabled until the preceding one is completed and the steps that are in progress are labeled with the approximate time (in minutes) it will take you to finish it. And whenever the work in a single step is done, it will be marked **Complete** on the summary page as shown in the following screenshot:

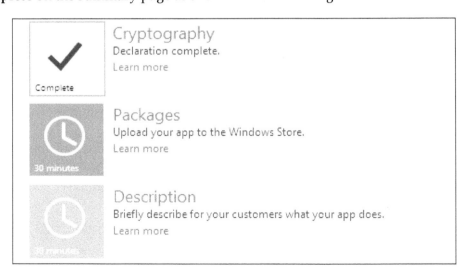

Submitting the app for certification

After all the steps are marked **Complete**, you can submit the app for certification. Once you click on **Submit for certification**, you will receive an e-mail notification that the Windows Store has received your app for certification. The dashboard will submit the app and you will be directed to the **Certification status** page. There, you can view the progress of the app during the certification process, which includes the following steps:

- **Pre-processing**: This step will check if you have entered all the required details that are needed to publish the app.

- **Security tests**: This step tests your app against viruses and malware.

- **Technical compliance**: This step involves the Windows App certification Kit to check if the app complies with the technical policies. The same assessment can be run locally using Visual Studio, which we will see shortly, before you upload your package.

- **Content compliance**: This step is done by testers from the Store team who will check if the contents available in the app comply with the content policies set by Microsoft.

- **Release**: This step involves releasing the app; it shouldn't take much time unless the publish date you've specified in **Selling details** is in the future, in which case the app will remain in this stage until that date arrives.

- **Signing and publishing**: This is the final step in the certification process. At this stage, the packages you submitted will be signed with a trusted certificate that matches the technical details of your developer account, thus guaranteeing for the potential customers and viewers that the app is certified by the Windows Store.

The following screenshot shows the certification process on Windows Store Dashboard:

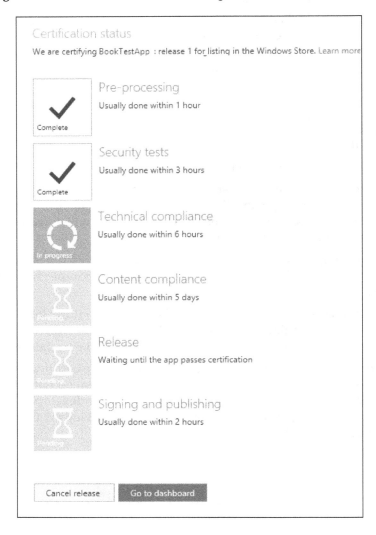

No need to wait on that page; you can click on the **Go to dashboard** button and you will be redirected to the **My apps** page. In the box containing the app you just submitted, you will notice that the **Edit** and **Delete** links are gone, and instead there is only the **Status** link, which will take you to the **Certification status** page. Additionally, a **Notifications** section will appear on this page and will list status notifications about the app you just submitted, for example:

BookTestApp: Release 1 submitted for certification.   **6/4/2013**

When the certification process is completed, you will be notified via e-mail with the result. Also, a notification will be added to the dashboard main page showing the result of the certification, either failed or succeeded, with a link to the certification report. In case the app fails, the certification reports will show you which part needs revisiting. Moreover, there are some resources to help you identify and fix the problems and errors that might arise during the certification process; these resources can be found at the *Windows Dev Center* page for Windows Store apps at the following location:

`http://msdn.microsoft.com/en-us/library/windows/apps/jj657968.aspx`

Also, you can always check your dashboard to check the status of your app during certification.

After the certification process is completed successfully, the app package will be published to the Store with all the relevant data that will be visible in your app listing page. This page can be accessed by millions of Windows 8 users who will in turn be able to find, install, and use your app.

Once the app has been published to the Store and it's up and running, you can start collecting telemetry data on how it is doing in the Store; these metrics include information on how many times the app has been launched, how long it has been running, and if it is crashing or encountering a JavaScript exception. Once you enable telemetry data collection, the Store will retrieve this info for your apps, analyze them, and summarize them in very informative reports on your dashboard.

Now that we have covered almost everything you need to know about the process of submitting your app to the Windows Store, let us see what is needed to be done in Visual Studio.

The Store within Visual Studio

Windows Store can be accessed from within Visual Studio using the **Store** menu. Not all the things that we did on the dashboard can be done here; a few very important functionalities such as app package creation are provided by this menu. The **Store** menu can be located under the **Project** item in the menu bar using Visual Studio 2012 Ultimate, or if you are using Visual Studio 2012 Express, you can find it directly in the menu bar, and it will appear only if you're working on a Windows Store project or solution.

We will get to see the commands provided by the **Store** menu in detail and the following is the screenshot that shows how the menu will look:

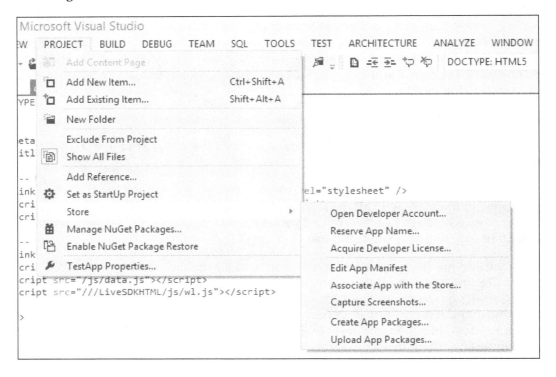

The command options in the **Store** menu are as follows:

- **Open Developer Account...**: This option will open a web page that directs you to *Windows Dev Center* for Windows Store apps, where you can obtain a developer account for the Store.

- **Reserve App Name...**: This option will direct you to your Windows Store Dashboard and specifically to the **Submit an app** page, where you can start with the first step, reserving an app name, as we saw earlier in *Chapter 8, Signing Users in*.

- **Acquire Developer License...**: This option will open up a dialog window that will prompt you to sign in with your Microsoft Account; after you sign in, it will retrieve your developer license or renew it if you already have one.

- **Edit App Manifest**: This option will open a tab with Manifest Designer, so you can edit the settings in the app's manifest file.

- **Associate App with the Store...**: This option will open a wizard-like window in Visual Studio, containing the steps needed to associate an app with the Store. The first step will prompt you to sign in; afterwards, the wizard will retrieve the apps registered with the Microsoft Account you used to sign in. Select an app and the wizard will automatically download the following values to the app's manifest file for the current project on the local computer:
    - ° Package's display name
    - ° Package's name
    - ° Publisher ID
    - ° Publisher's display name

- **Capture Screenshot...**: This option will build the current app project and launch it in the simulator instead of the start screen. Once the simulator opens, you can use the **Copy screenshot** button on the simulator sidebar. This button will be used to take a screenshot of the running app that will save this image as a .png file.

- **Create App Package...**: This option will open a window containing the **Create App Packages** wizard that we will see shortly.

- **Upload App Package...**: This option will open a browser that directs you to the Release Summary page in the Windows Store Dashboard, if your Store account is all set and your app is registered. Otherwise, it will just take you to the sign-in page. In the Release Summary page, you can select **Packages** and from there upload your app package.

Creating an App Package

One of the most important utilities in the **Store** menu is the app package creation, which will build and create a package for the app that we can upload to the Store at a later stage. This package is consistent with all the app-specific and developer-specific details that the Store requires. Moreover, the developers do not have to worry about any of the intricacies of the whole package-creation process, which is abstracted for us and available via a wizard-link window.

In the **Create App Packages** wizard, we can create an app package for the Windows Store directly, or create the one to be used for testing or local distribution. This wizard will prompt you to specify metadata for the app package.

The following screenshot shows the first two steps involved in this process:

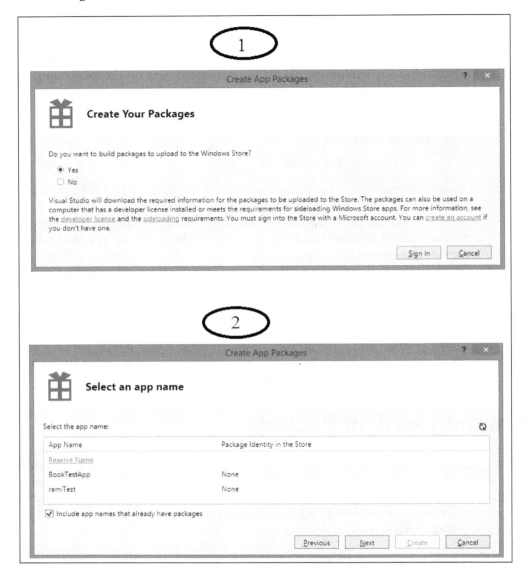

In the first step, the wizard will ask you if you want to build packages to upload to the Windows Store; choose **Yes** if you want to build a package for the Store or choose **No** if you want a package for testing and local use. Taking the first scenario in consideration, click on **Sign In** to proceed and complete the sign-in process using your Microsoft Account.

After a successful sign-in, the wizard will prompt you to **select the app name** (step 2 of the preceding screenshot) either by clicking on the apps listed in the wizard or choosing the **Reserve Name** link that will direct you to the Windows Store Dashboard to complete the process and reserve a new app name. The following screenshot shows step 3 and step 4:

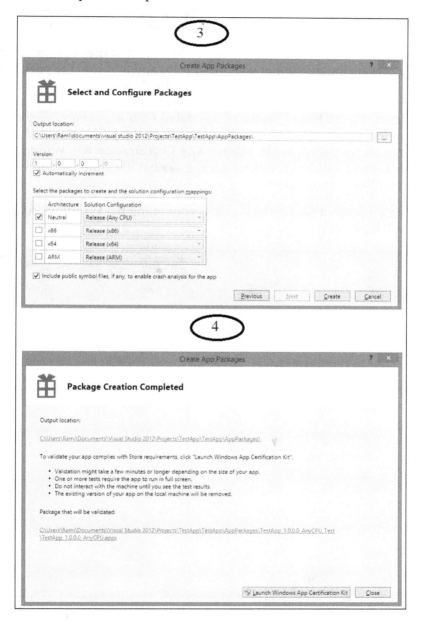

Step 3 contains the **Select and Configure Packages** section in which we will select **Output location** that points to where the package files will be created. Also, in this section we can enter a version number for this package or chose to make it auto-increment each time we package the app. Additionally, we can select the build configuration we want for the package from the **Neutral**, **ARM**, **x64**, and **x86** options and by default, the current active project platform will be selected and a package will be produced for each configuration type selected.

The last option in this section is the **Include public symbol files** option. Selecting this option will generate the public symbols files (**.pdb**) and add it to the package, which will help the store later in analyzing your app and will be used to map crashes of your app. Finally, click on **Create** and wait while the packaging is being processed. Once completed, the **Package Creation Completed** section appears (step 4) and will show **Output location** as a link that will direct you to the package files. Also, there is a button to directly launch the **Windows App Certification Kit**. **Windows App Certification Kit** will validate the app package against the Store requirements and generate a report of the validation.

The following screenshot shows the window containing the **Windows App Certification Kit** process:

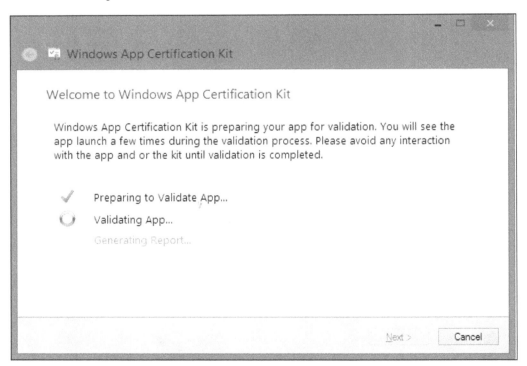

Alternatively, there is a second scenario for creating an app package but it is more aimed at testing, which is identical to the process we just saw except that you have to choose **No** in the first page on the wizard and there is no need to sign-in with the Microsoft Account. This option will end the wizard when the package creation has completed and display the link to the output folder but you will not be able to launch the **Windows App Certification Kit**. The packages created with this option can only be used on a computer that has a developer license installed. This scenario will be used more often since the package for the Store should ideally be tested locally first. After creating the app package for testing or local distribution, you can install it on a local machine or device.

Let's install the package locally. Start the **Create App Packages** wizard; choose **No** in the first step, complete the wizard, and find files of the app package just created in the output folder that you specified for the package location. Name this as `PackageName_Test`. This folder will contain an `.appx` file, a security certificate, a Windows PowerShell script, and other files. The Windows PowerShell script generated with the app package will be used to install the package for testing. Navigate to the **Output** folder and install the app package. Locate and select the script file named `Add-AppDevPackage`, and then right-click and choose **Run with PowerShell** as shown in the following screenshot:

Run the script and it will perform the following steps:

1. It displays information about **Execution Policy Change** and prompts about changing the execution policy. Enter `Y` to continue.

2. It checks if you have a developer license; in case there wasn't any script, it will prompt you to get one.

3. It checks and verifies whether the app package and the required certificates are present; if any item is missing, you will be notified to install them before the developer package is installed.

4. It checks for and installs any dependency packages such as the `WinJS` library.

5. It displays the message **Success: Your package was successfully installed**.

6. Press *Enter* to continue and the window will close.

The aforementioned steps are shown in the following screenshot:

```
Execution Policy Change
The execution policy helps protect you from scripts that you do not trust. Changing the execution policy might expose
you to the security risks described in the about_Execution_Policies help topic at
http://go.microsoft.com/fwlink/?LinkID=135170. Do you want to change the execution policy?
[Y] Yes  [N] No  [S] Suspend  [?] Help (default is "Y"): y
Found package: C:\Users\Rami\Documents\Visual Studio 2012\Projects\TestApp\TestApp\AppPackages\TestApp_1.0.0.4_AnyCPU_De
bug_Test\TestApp_1.0.0.4_AnyCPU_Debug.appx

Installing package...
Found dependency package(s):
C:\Users\Rami\Documents\Visual Studio 2012\Projects\TestApp\TestApp\AppPackages\TestApp_1.0.0.4_AnyCPU_Debug_Test\Depen
dencies\Microsoft.WinJS.1.0.appx

Success: Your package was successfully installed.
Press Enter to continue...:
```

Once the script has completed successfully, you can look for your app on the **Start** screen and start it.

 Note that for users who are on a network and don't have permission to access the directory where the Add-AppDevPackage PowerShell script file is located, an error message might appear. This issue can be solved by simply copying the contents of the output folder to the local machine before running the script. Also, for any security-related issues, you might want to consult the Windows Developer Center for solutions.

Summary

In this chapter, we saw the ins and outs of the Windows Store Dashboard and we covered the steps of the app submission process leading to the publishing of the app in the Store. We also learned about the **Store** menu in Visual Studio and the options it provides to interact with the dashboard. Moreover, we learned how to create app packages and how to deploy the app locally for testing.

In the next chapter we will have a sneak peak at the other side of the coin, developing Windows 8 apps with XAML, and understand how similar it is to developing apps with JavaScript, thereby showing you the power of developing apps for Windows 8 with multiple programming languages.

11
Developing Apps with XAML

Developing Windows Store apps is not exclusive to HTML5 and JavaScript. Microsoft offers other choices with **Extensible Application Markup Language** (**XAML**) and .NET, thus targeting a broader range of developers and expertise to develop for the Store. Whatever your background is, whether web or Windows development, there is a place for you—a starting point—because the road map to the Windows Store will be the same regardless of your choice of programming language. In the previous chapters, we have been learning how to develop apps and features with HTML5 and JavaScript. But in this chapter, we will learn about other platforms and programming languages available for developers. We will also cover the basics of creating an app with XAML/C#.

Creating apps with different platforms

One of the paramount advances with Windows 8 is that you can develop apps with more than one framework and programming language, targeting both web and Windows developers. Moreover, developers can build on and leverage their existing programming skills and knowledge to create Windows Store apps, and will not necessarily have to acquire a completely new set of skills.

Web developers will be able to utilize their HTML5, CSS3, and JavaScript skills and can even port existing websites easily into a Store app, while Windows developers, familiar with Microsoft .NET Framework and Silverlight, can put into action their XAML, C#, and Visual Basic skills. Additionally, Windows 8 targets developers who are familiar with the C++ syntax and native libraries by providing the opportunity to create Windows Store apps in Visual C++/XAML. Moreover, C++, you can create Direct2D and Direct3D apps. In summary, we have the XAML markup with C#, VB.NET, and C++, and to top it, Visual Studio 2012 provides project templates and Intellisense support for all these programming languages.

The same app can be built with either XAML or HTML5, and when deployed and run, both versions will run in an identical manner. Everything that we have learned to do in the previous chapters with JavaScript and HTML5 for Windows Store apps, from functionalities to features, can be done with C#, VB.Net, and XAML. The choice of the programming language to be used is based on personal preference, background experience, and language familiarity more than anything else. Both choices will require some level of learning. Web developers who are familiar with the HTML markup, styling with CSS, and functionality with JavaScript, will need to learn about WinJS-specific JavaScript functions and HTML data attributes and classes. Also, developers who have experience with XAML will notice a great deal of familiarity with WPF and Silverlight, but will have to learn about developing for the Windows Store design and functionality. However, as I mentioned, the learning curve is minimal when you are commencing Windows Store development with a familiar territory.

Introducing XAML apps

The roadmap for Windows Store apps using XAML is the same as that for Store apps using JavaScript, beginning with tools and acquiring a developer license through the design guidelines to planning the app and finishing with packaging and publishing the app to the Store.

Let's create a basic Windows Store app using XAML and compare it with an app made using HTML5. In Visual Studio, from the top menu, navigate to **File | New Project**. In the **New Project** dialog window, choose your preferred programming language from the left pane under **Installed | Templates** and then select **Windows Store**. Next, we select one of the listed project templates for a Windows Store app and enter a name for it in the **Name:** textbox. I will choose **Visual C#** for this demonstration; feel free to go with **Visual Basic** or **Visual C++**. Finally, click on **OK** to create the project: The following screenshot shows the entire process as discussed:

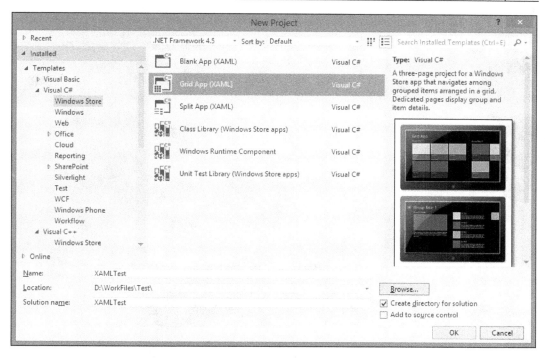

The preceding screenshot shows the following Windows Store app templates provided with XAML: **Blank App (XAML)**, **Grid App (XAML)**, and **Split App (XAML)**.

- **Blank App (XAML)**: This template provides an empty Windows Store app that will compile and run, but contains no user interface controls or data. When it runs an app based on this template, it will only show a black screen that contains a placeholder text.

- **Grid App (XAML)**: This template provides an app that enables users to browse through categories and dive into the details of the content that falls under each category. A few good examples for this template include shopping apps, news apps, and photo or video apps. The **Grid App (XAML)** template starts with a landing home page that will display a list of groups or categories. A single group is a named set of items; for example, a group of news articles named Sports News. When the user selects one group, the app opens the group details page, which in turn displays a list of items that the group contains on the right-hand side. Consequently, when the user selects a single item on either the home page or the group details page, the app will open a page that shows the item details.

The following screenshot shows a sample home page of **Grid App (XAML)**:

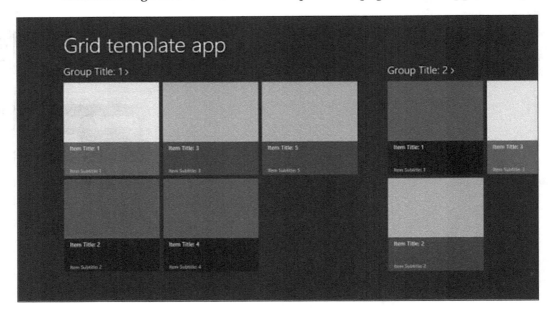

- **Split App (XAML)**: This template provides an app that enables users to browse through categories to find specific content similar to a **Grid App (XAML)** template; however, with the **Split App (XAML)** template, users can view a list of items and item details in the same page in a two-column split view. This split view enables all users to switch among the items rapidly. Examples for the usage of this template include news readers or an e-mail app. This template starts with a landing home page that shows a list of groups. When the user selects a group, the app will open a split-view page. The following screenshot shows a sample split-view page:

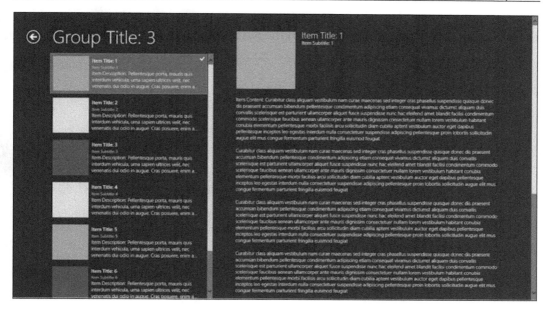

These three project templates are similar to the ones provided in a Windows Store JavaScript project, but the latter provides two additional templates, the **Fixed Layout App** and the **Navigation App**.

We'll start with the **Blank App (XAML)** template, which contains the minimal project files required to run the app. The **Blank App (XAML)** template creates an empty Windows Store app that contains no user interface, but will compile and run. Once the blank app has been created, navigate to **Solution Explorer** on the right-hand side of Visual Studio and expand the list of project files to see the default files that are created with this template.

The following screenshot shows the contents of **Solution Explorer** to the right and the `MainPage.xaml` file, when opened in the XAML text editor, to the left:

The project we just created contains the following folders and files, which are indispensable to all Windows Store apps using C# or Visual Basic:

- `Properties`: This folder contains the app assembly information.

- `References`: This folder contains the project references files and by default, has the following two SDK references: **.NET for Windows Store apps** and **Windows**.

- `Assets`: This folder contains the following images:
  - Large and small logo images of sizes 150 x 150 px and 30 x 30 px, respectively.
  - The **SplashScreen** image.
  - The **StoreLogo** image of size 50 x 50 px.

- `Common`: This folder contains the common shared resources in the app such as the `StandardStyles.xaml` file, which provides a set of default styles that gives the app its Windows 8 look and feel. In addition, this folder will contain the files for the utility and helper classes.

This template also includes the following `.xaml` page files:

- `App.xaml`: This is the main app file that is required to display the user interface and is first loaded when the app runs. This page declares resources that are shared across the app, such as styles, and provides the markup for the content host. This page is similar to what the `default.html` page represents in apps using JavaScript.

- `App.xaml.cs`: This is the code-behind file for `App.xaml` and contains the code that handles the global app-specific behavior and events, such as app launching and suspending. This file is similar to what the `default.js` file represents in apps using JavaScript.

- `MainPage.xaml`: This is the default startup page of the app and contains the minimal XAML markup and code to instantiate a page.

- `MainPage.xaml.cs`: This is the code-behind file corresponding to the `MainPage.xaml` file.

Finally, there is the manifest file, `Package.appxmanifest`, which contains the app description and settings identical to the one in JavaScript templates.

 Microsoft recommends to not remove the files in the `Common` folder. Also, it can neither be renamed nor modified because this results in a build error. If there is a necessity to modify these files, you can create a copy of the original file and then modify the copy instead.

Those who haven't heard of XAML before might be lost by now and wondering about the syntax you just saw in the app and the `MainPage.xaml` files. XAML has a basic syntax that is built on XML. When stripped down, an XAML document is an XML document that shows a hierarchical relationship between objects, and to be considered valid, it must also be a valid XML document. XAML files have a `.xaml` filename extension, and each XAML file is associated with a code-behind file that contains the code that will handle events, and manipulate objects and UI elements that were created or declared in XAML. The code-behind file joined with the XAML page's partial class makes a complete class. This is similar to the concept of ASP.NET web pages with `.aspx` files containing the markup and code-behind in the `.cs` or `.vb` files. Also, XAML files can be opened and edited in Microsoft Expression Blend. If you are new to XAML, don't worry much about the syntax because Visual Studio helps you write a valid markup by providing autocompletion hints and suggestion lists, and you will learn the syntax along the way.

Using XAML markup, we can create UI elements just like we do using HTML but with a different syntax. Let's add the following UI elements inside the `Grid` element in the `MainPage.xaml` file with the following syntax:

```
<TextBlock x:Name="pageTitle" Text="Test XAML App" ></TextBlock>
<TextBox Text="Input text here..." />
<CheckBox Content="Yes"/>
```

The preceding code listing shows the following properties: `x:Name`, which specifies the name assigned to the `TextBlock` element; `Text`, which specifies the data as text that will be filled in this element; and `Content`, which is similar to `Text` but specifies the data as text that will show next to a `CheckBox` element.

The first line in the code listing declares a basic `TextBlock` element, which is similar to a `label` element in HTML. We give this element a name and enter a value for its `Text` property. The second element is `Textbox` with a `Text` value, and the third one is a `Checkbox` element with the `Content` value. You can either write the syntax manually or choose a control from those listed in the **Toolbox** pane and drag it directly to the XAML text editor or the design surface, which are both visible in a split view.

In the designer window, you can manipulate these UI controls and arrange their positioning on the window as shown in the following screenshot:

You will notice that manipulating the controls in the **Design** pane reflects on the syntax in the **XAML** pane below it, as new properties are being set for the elements and existing ones are being changed. If you run the app now, you will see a black screen containing the three elements we just added to the `MainPage.xaml` file.

The `MainPage.xaml` file contains the minimum markup and code needed to run the page, but lacks all the additional code and classes that implement important features in a Windows Store app, such as adapting to changes in view and handling different states of the app. Fortunately, the other page templates provided by Visual Studio, such as the Basic Page template, include the code and helper classes that help you implement these features. For this purpose, we typically replace that empty `MainPage` template with one of the other page templates while working with a Blank App (XAML) project. In order to replace the `MainPage.xaml` file, right-click on it in **Solution Explorer** and click on **Delete**. Then, right-click on the project root node and click on **Add New Item**, which will open up a dialog window. From there, select the **Windows Store** template type under **Visual C#** (or Visual Basic if you chose a different template at the start of the example). Next, select **Basic Page** and give it the name `MainPage.xaml`, otherwise the project will not build correctly. The following screenshot illustrates the procedure:

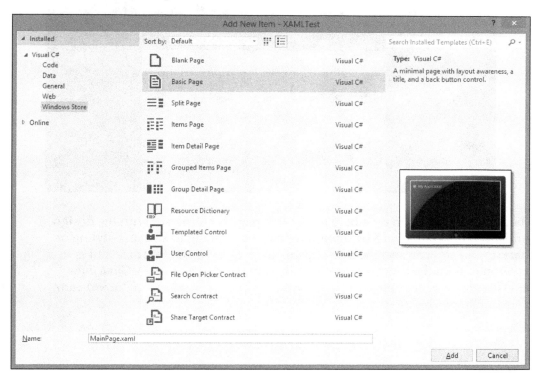

Then, click on **Add**. If this is the first time you have added a new page different from the **Blank Page** template to the **Blank App (XAML)** template, a message dialog will be displayed with the warning, **This addition depends on files that are missing from your project**. Click on **Yes** to add the missing files automatically. The XAML and code-behind files for this page are added to the project, and if you expand the Common folder, you will notice that the folder that first contained a single file, StandardStyles.xaml, is now populated with code files that contain several helper and utility classes. The newly added page will not show up in the designer until you build the project/solution, so it compiles the helper classes the page depends on. Let's see how the app looks like after this change; press *F5* to build and run the app in debugging mode.

Once it's run, the app will appear as a black screen containing the title **My Application**, as shown in the following screenshot:

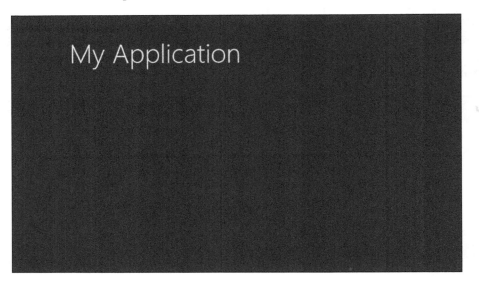

The important thing to note here is that this page is consistent with the design guidelines for Windows 8 by default, without us having to add any styling or markup. As you can see, the title appears to be of the same font size and is positioned with the exact margins specified in the *Windows 8 UX Guidelines for Windows Store apps* page (http://www.microsoft.com/en-in/download/details.aspx?id=30704).

Adding a title, theme color, and content

Let's modify this minimal app by adding a title and changing its theme color. Then, we'll add a simple text and write some code to handle a basic button-click event.

1. To change the title of this app, perform the following steps:

    1. Open the `MainPage.xaml` file.

    2. In the **XAML** designer pane, select the title **My Application** and either right-click on it and select **Edit Text** or change the value of the `Text` property found in the **Properties** window under `Common`. If it is not shown by default, the **Property** window should be located on the left-hand side of Visual Studio below the **Solution Explorer** panel.

2. To change the theme color of this app, perform the following steps. Similar to what we had done in the app using JavaScript, we can switch between dark and light themes here as well. In the app using JavaScript, there were two CSS files, `ui-dark.css` and `ui-light.css`, referenced in the `default.html` page. In apps using XAML, switching between the two themes is done in the `App.xaml` file as follows:

    1. Open the `App.xaml` file.

    2. Go to the `<Application>` tag and add the `RequestedTheme` property before the closing of the tag.

    3. Click within the quotes of the tag, and Visual Studio's Intellisense will prompt you with two property values: **Light** and **Dark**. Choose **Light** and the `<Application>` tag will look as follows:

        ```
        <Application
        x:Class="App1.App"
            xmlns="http://schemas.microsoft.com/winfx/2006/xaml/
        presentation"
            xmlns:x="http://schemas.microsoft.com/winfx/2006/xaml"
            xmlns:local="using:App1"
            RequestedTheme="Light">
        ```

    4. Run the app to see the difference.

3. Now to add some UI content, open the `MainPage.xaml` file and locate the root `Grid` element and the `<VisualStateManager.VisualStateGroups>` tag inside it. Add the following XAML code snippet just before this tag:

    ```
    <StackPanel Grid.Row="1" Margin="120,30,0,0">
      <TextBlock Text="Is this your first XAML App?"/>
    ```

```
<StackPanel Orientation="Horizontal" Margin="0,20,0,20">
  <TextBox x:Name="answerInput" Width="360"
    HorizontalAlignment="Left"/>
  <Button Content="Post My Answer"/>
</StackPanel>
<TextBlock x:Name="myAnswer"/>
</StackPanel>
```

The preceding XAML code declares a `StackPanel` control that holds UI controls inside it (think of it as a `div` element). Inside this, we add a `TextBlock` element and assign its `Text` property a value, and then we nest a `StackPanel` control inside the parent `StackPanel` (`div` inside a `div` element). This `StackPanel` element will hold two controls: a `TextBox` element to enter the input values that we assign for its `width` and `HorizontalAlignment` properties, and a `Button` control to which we assign a value for its `Content` property. Finally, add another empty `TextBlock` element outside the inner `StackPanel` element.

Run the app and it will look like the following screenshot:

4. Lastly, let's add some functionality with an event handler for the button we declared in the markup, as enlisted in the following steps:

    1. Click on the **Post My Answer** button in either the XAML designer or the text editor, and it will show in the **Properties** window.

    2. In the **Properties** window, locate and click on the **Events** button on the top-left area.

    3. Locate the **Click** event at the top of the list and double-click or press *Enter* in the textbox provided.

This will create the event handler method. Display it in the code editor of the file `MainPage.xaml.cs`.

The following screenshot shows the process:

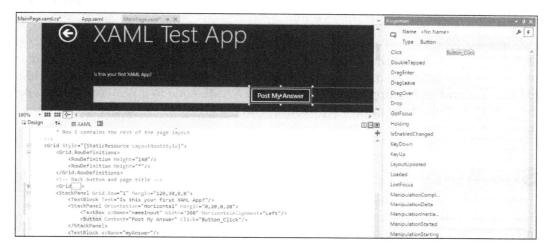

The autogenerated event handler comes up with the name `Button_Click` (if the button had a value for its `name` property, the event handler would have looked something like `ButtonName_Click`). The method will look as follows:

```
private void Button_Click(object sender, RoutedEventArgs e)
{
}
```

Let's add simple code that gets the text entered in the input textbox and displays it in the empty `TextBlock` named `myAnswer`. The code will look as follows:

```
private void Button_Click(object sender, RoutedEventArgs e)
{
    myAnswer.Text = answerInput.Text;
}
```

If we go back to the XAML editor, we'll see that the `Click` event handler was added to the `Button` element like this:

```
<Button Content="Post My Answer" Click="Button_Click"/>
```

Run the app now, enter some text in the textbox, and test the button. Once clicked, it will output whatever is inside the textbox to the screen.

There is much more to XAML than this simple demo, and the previous example merely shows us how we can start with a very basic app and build up content and functionality. XAML is not that hard once we become familiar with it; as with any other programming language, we will need practice. However, the choice between XAML and HTML5 is completely yours.

One of the advantages of developing Windows Store apps with XAML is the ability to migrate **Windows Phone 7** apps to Windows 8 using the guide provided by Microsoft to help you make the conversion. Likewise, Microsoft provides a guide to help you port an existing Silverlight or WPF/XAML code to a Windows Store app using XAML. Both these guides are available on the *Windows Phone Dev Center* page (`http://developer.windowsphone.com/en-us`).

Summary

In this chapter, we have learned about different choices offered by Windows 8 for developers. Additionally, we were introduced to the XAML language and syntax in Windows Store apps.

We also covered how to start developing Windows Store apps using XAML and how it differs from developing using JavaScript, which gave us a heads-up on what to expect when we want to develop with either languages.

Finally, we created a minimal app and added to it some basic UI content and functionality using the XAML markup.

In this book, we introduced new features in HTML5 and CSS3 and then learned how these features are being implemented in a Windows Store app. We also covered the JavaScript controls' functionalities, which are specific to the Windows Store app. After this, we learned how to create a basic JavaScript app and how to quick-start developing Windows Store apps with JavaScript. Further, we got to learn about some of the important features of the apps and how to implement these features. We started by retrieving data and displaying it using WinJS controls. Then, we got introduced to the view states of the app and how to make the app respond to changes in these view states. Afterward, we covered the tiles in Windows 8 and learned how to add live tiles and send notifications to the app. Also, we learned how to integrate the app with Windows Live services to enable authentication and sign-in for users using their e-mail accounts. We also learned about the app bar in a Windows Store app and how to add buttons to it. Finally, we got introduced to the Windows Store and learned all about packaging and publishing the app to the store.

Index

JavaScript, using 14, 15
mediagroup attribute 11
media queries 39
MediaRule 39
media type 39
Menu control 49
metadata value 11
min attribute 19
min-content keyword 33
minmax(a,b) keyword 33
minRating attribute 51
month attribute 16
MSDN website
  URL 53
ms-stream value 47
multiple attribute 16
muted attribute 11
myVideo element 14

N

name property 75, 157
nav element 24
Navigation App 58, 149
none value 11
note feature 133
notifications
  about 99-104
  sending 104-107
notifications delivery methods
  Local method 104
  Periodic method 105
  Push method 105
  Scheduled method 104
number attribute 16

O

OAuth 110
OAuth 2.0 110
objects
  asynchronous programming 41-44
onactivated event 66
onactivated handler 66
Open Authentication. *See* OAuth

orientation preference
  values 90

P

package.appxmanifest 63
Package.appxmanifest file 151
packages 133
Page Control 59
PageControl object 128
password option 48
pattern attribute 19
pause() method 14
People app 103, 104
Periodic method 105
person object 74, 75
Pin to start command button 127, 128
Pin to Start option 103
placement property 128
play() method 14
Post My Answer button 156
poster attribute 13
preceding selectors
  Adjacent Sibling selector 28
  Descendant selector 27
  Direct Descendant selector 28
  General Sibling selector 29
preload attribute
  about 11
  auto value 11
  metadata value 11
  none value 11
privacy policy feature 134
progress element 17
Promise 42
Promise object 44, 47
Property window 155
pseudo-class selector 29
pseudo-elements
  ::after 30
  ::before 30
  ::first-letter 30
  ::first-line 30
  ::selection 30
pseudo-element selector 29, 30

Push method 105

Q

query() 45
QueryCollection
  addClass method 46
  children method 46
  clearStyle method 46
  getAttribute method 46
  hasClass method 46
  query(query) method 46
  removeClass method 46
  removeEventListener method 46
  setAttribute method 46
  setStyle method 46
  toggleClass method 46
QueryCollection object 45
querySelectorAll() function 45
querySelector() function 45

R

range attribute 16
Rating control 49
readTextAsync(file) function 76
readTextAsync(file) method 76
release date option 132
render method 79
Representational State Transfer. *See* REST
RequestedTheme property 155
required attribute 17-19, 25
responseType option
  about 47
  arraybuffer value 47
  blob value 47
  document value 47
  json value 47
  ms-stream value 47
  text value 47
REST 110

S

Sample App Pack 54
Scheduled method 104

screenshot feature 133
search attribute 16
Search Contract 59
section option
  about 126
  global section 126
  selection section 126
Secure Sockets Layer (SSL) 133
selection section 126
selector 23
selling details
  accessibility option 132
  app category option 132
  app price tier option 132
  app subcategory option 132
  free trial period option 132
  hardware requirements option 132
  market option 132
  release date option 132
semantic elements
  <address> tag 8
  <article> tag 8
  <aside> tag 8
  <footer> tag 8
  <header> tag 8
  <nav> tag 8
  <section> tag 8
  about 8
semantic zoom 93-96
SemanticZoom control 49, 95
services 132
setAttribute method 20
setNameBtn button 75
Share Target Contract 60
Sign in button 117, 122
Single Sign-on (SSO) 54
snapped and fill layouts 59
snapped view 88
Software Development Kit (SDK) 109
sortedList method 82
SortedListProjection object 81
span element 74
Split App 57
Split App (XAML) 148
src attribute 11
StackPanel element 156

Thank you for buying
Developing Windows Store Apps with HTML5 and JavaScript

About Packt Publishing

Packt, pronounced 'packed', published its first book "Mastering phpMyAdmin for Effective MySQL Management" in April 2004 and subsequently continued to specialize in publishing highly focused books on specific technologies and solutions.

Our books and publications share the experiences of your fellow IT professionals in adapting and customizing today's systems, applications, and frameworks. Our solution based books give you the knowledge and power to customize the software and technologies you're using to get the job done. Packt books are more specific and less general than the IT books you have seen in the past. Our unique business model allows us to bring you more focused information, giving you more of what you need to know, and less of what you don't.

Packt is a modern, yet unique publishing company, which focuses on producing quality, cutting-edge books for communities of developers, administrators, and newbies alike. For more information, please visit our website: www.packtpub.com.

About Packt Enterprise

In 2010, Packt launched two new brands, Packt Enterprise and Packt Open Source, in order to continue its focus on specialization. This book is part of the Packt Enterprise brand, home to books published on enterprise software – software created by major vendors, including (but not limited to) IBM, Microsoft and Oracle, often for use in other corporations. Its titles will offer information relevant to a range of users of this software, including administrators, developers, architects, and end users.

Writing for Packt

We welcome all inquiries from people who are interested in authoring. Book proposals should be sent to author@packtpub.com. If your book idea is still at an early stage and you would like to discuss it first before writing a formal book proposal, contact us; one of our commissioning editors will get in touch with you.

We're not just looking for published authors; if you have strong technical skills but no writing experience, our experienced editors can help you develop a writing career, or simply get some additional reward for your expertise.

HTML5 Enterprise Application Development

HTML5 Enterprise Application Development

ISBN: 978-1-849685-68-9   Paperback: 332 pages

A step-by-step practical introduction to HTML5 through the building of a real-world application, including common development practices

1. Learn the most useful HTML5 features by developing a real-world application

2. Detailed solutions to most common problems presented in an enterprise application development

3. Discover the most up-to-date development tips, tendencies, and trending libraries and tools

HTML5 Web Application Development By Example

HTML5 Web Application Development By Example Beginner's Guide

ISBN: 978-1-849695-94-7   Paperback: 276 pages

Learn how to build rich, interactive web applications from the ground up using HMTL5, CSS3, and jQuery

1. Packed with example applications that show you how to create rich, interactive applications and games.

2. Shows you how to use the most popular and widely supported features of HTML5

3. Full of tips and tricks for writing more efficient and robust code while avoiding some of the pitfalls inherent to JavaScript

Please check **www.PacktPub.com** for information on our titles

Designing Next Generation Web Projects with CSS3

ISBN: 978-1-849693-26-4   Paperback: 288 pages

A practical guide to the usage of CSS3 – a journey through properties, tools, and techniques to better understand CSS3

1. CSS3 properties and techniques have been applied to complete web projects

2. Explains tools to deal with CSS increasing in complexity, such as experimental vendor prefixes

3. Fast and concise style focused primarily on practical aspects like implementation techniques and fallback strategies

Windows Phone 8 Game Development

ISBN: 978-1-849696-80-7   Paperback: 270 pages

A practical guide to creating games for the Windows Phone 8 platform using 2D and 3D graphics, sensors, geolocation, augmented reality, social networks, and web services

1. Create a 3D game for the Windows Phone 8 platform

2. Combine native and managed development approaches

3. Discover how to use a range of inputs, including sensors

Please check **www.PacktPub.com** for information on our titles